Forgotten All-Star

A Biography of Gardner Fox

Jennifer DeRoss

Pulp Hero Press
The Most Dangerous Books on Earth
www.PulpHeroPress.com

Pulp Hero Press publishes its books in a variety of print and electronic formats. Some content that appears in one format may not appear in another.

Editor: Bob McLain
Layout: Artisanal Text
Special thanks to Roy Thomas
ISBN 978-1-68390-200-3
Printed in the United States of America

Pulp Hero Press | www.PulpHeroPress.com
Address queries to bob@pulpheropress.com

Contents

Introduction   *v*

Timeline   *xv*

Family Tree   *xvii*

PART ONE

CHAPTER ONE
The Youthful Fox   3

CHAPTER TWO
Courage in the College Years   13

CHAPTER THREE
The Trials and Triumphs of Adulthood   23

PART TWO

CHAPTER FOUR
Fox's First Steps into the World of
Professional Writing   33

CHAPTER FIVE
The Official Beginning of Fox's Comics Career   49

PART THREE

CHAPTER SIX
An All-Star Humanitarian During War   63

CHAPTER SEVEN
The Wonder Woman Issue   77

PART FOUR

CHAPTER EIGHT
The Gilding Begins to Dull   95

CHAPTER NINE
The Comics Code Strikes a Blow   113

PART FIVE

CHAPTER TEN
Now Featuring Justice! On Earth 2!   127

CHAPTER ELEVEN
Meanwhile, Marvel's Massive Emergence   145

CHAPTER TWELVE
Fame!   153

CHAPTER THIRTEEN
And Defeat   167

PART SIX

CHAPTER FOURTEEN
Fox Finally Finds His Freedom   179

CHAPTER FIFTEEN
Garnering a Grasp on Gardner Fox's Legacy   199

End Notes   207
Acknowledgments   219
About the Author   221

Introduction

Where can one start when describing the life of Gardner Fox?

His writing career spanned more than four decades, starting before Superman was published in the late 1930s all the way to the start of the creator-owned independent comics boom in the mid-1980s. He took part in the creation of many characters in the Golden Age, and their reinvention in the Silver Age. He was also the writer at the helm when groups of those characters were put on teams together. He was at the center of too many firsts to list, with perhaps the two biggest being when he brought the concept of the multiverse to the DC[1] universe, and when he wrote the first multi-issue crossover event.

If you love stories and characters from Golden and Silver Age comics, there is a good chance you love Gardner Fox. It is possible you love his stories without knowing he is the man behind them because he is not as much of a household name when compared to other comic writers from the era like Jerry Siegel and Bill Finger. His versatility allowed him to write stories in many different genres including westerns, historical fiction, sword-and-sorcery, horror, science-fiction, and soft-porn, as well as the action-adventure genre that includes most super-hero comics. On top of all that, he was writing short stories and novels at the same time.

Exemplifying his excellence, he won several awards both while he was alive and posthumously. Between 1961 and 1965, Gardner Fox won five Alley Awards and was nominated for many others. He also attended events where he received the Inkpot Award and the Jules Verne Award. After his death, he won even more. In 1998, he achieved a Harvey Award for his career body of work and was entered into the Jack Kirby Hall of

Fame. A year later, he was inducted into the Eisner Award Hall of Fame as well. Finally, and perhaps most notably, he was given the Bill Finger Award for Excellence in Comic Book Writing in 2007. Still, work on Gardner Fox remains shockingly sparse.

So why has the general populace never heard of him?

As much as Gardner Fox is foundational to much of DC, and to the comic industry as a whole, he is far too easily overlooked. Admittedly, his imaginative writing is not necessarily of the first rank in the literary sense, but there are a lot of other factors at play. As a married college graduate with two degrees, Fox started writing comics from a different social position than most at the time. He wasn't there for many of the events that have become industry-related stories; mostly, he worked from the comfort of home. He was a stoic, methodical man with a quiet smile and he did not fight to include his name on his works. Fanzines did some of the corrective labor of identifying creators, but that didn't start until the 1960s. As far as the comics themselves went, it wasn't until 1961's *Brave and the Bold* #35 that Gardner Fox would have his biographical information included in the letters section. DC still does not promote their own history in the way companies like Marvel do, and, when they do, their artists and editors tend to get more attention than their writers.

An additional reason work on Gardner Fox remains difficult to find is the Fox canon itself. Gardner Fox's prodigious output is the second largest in comic book history, totaling more than 4,200 stories written for a wide range of publishers, from the larger DC and Marvel to the smaller Columbia and Eclipse. That massive number does not include any of the short stories or the over 160 novels he wrote. These numbers are hard to calculate not only because he was so prolific, but also because he would use many pseudonyms, both male and female. There are a few different reasons given for this. In a letter to Jerry Bails, he said his name was "owned" by Gold Medal and Crest books. This meant that he had to use a pseudonym to write for other publishers like Signet, Monarch, and Avon.[2]

Additionally, Fox believed some publishers actually preferred the pseudonyms.[3] His family proved unable to shed any light on why he used so many different aliases. Regardless of the specific reason, one can see how it was a logical decision for Fox. He wasn't used to getting his name on his work anyway, and the work he did was sometimes at odds with what society deemed appropriate.

As a devout Catholic, he might have felt the stakes were higher for him. This is not to say he felt ashamed of his work; but he knew the societal impressions placed on some of it.

His list of pen names is huge. Some of them are names based on family members such as Jefferson Cooper, which includes both a nod to his son's name and his own middle name, or Lynna Cooper, which is a nod to the name his wife and daughter share along with his middle name once again. Not all of them are as obvious, but many are done as an homage to his favorite writers. Bart Somers, Kevin Matthews, and Rod Grey are probably his most well known.

Given how complicated and multiplicitous Gardner Fox's plethora of work is, my biographical sources were key in defining the limits of this project. My primary source was the Gardner Fox Collection located at the University of Oregon Libraries, Special Collections and University Archives.

Starting in the late 1960s, the curators at the university were requesting archival materials from various authors to develop and increase their popular literature collection. The University of Oregon reached out to Fox's literary agent, August Lenniger, and he suggested Fox donate his files as a tax write-off. After thinking about it, Fox agreed with the plan and donated materials both in 1967 and 1980. He would eventually donate 65 containers worth of materials equaling 31.25 linear feet[4] The collection features a breadth of materials including business correspondence, fan letters, scripts, research notebooks, comic books, periodicals, fanzines, paperback books, and miscellany.

Along with the Gardner Fox Collection, I made use of three other archives. St. John's University Archives was essential for finding information about Gardner Fox's college years. The Historical Society of Cheshire County and the Keene Public Library provided many details about his sister, Kay Fox, and daughter, Lynda Fox Cohen, that were relevant to Gardner Fox's life. In addition to doing archival work, I have reached out to a number of people in the comic industry who were kind enough to help. Among these, the help Roy Thomas provided has been extraordinary. He copied stacks of relevant letters and emailed me many other sources as well as simply being there to answer questions. Timothy Truman, Michael T. Gilbert, and Mike Barr were also valuable sources.

Gardner Fox's family has been crucial to this project as well, with Greg and Theresa Fox being two of the most important touchstones. I could not have done this without them. Finally, I spent a lot of time digging through fanzines and newspapers as well as reading massive amounts of Gardner Fox's work.

My through line is obviously punctuated by the major events in Gardner Fox's life, but I also include an analysis of some of his major works that fit within my narrative. The lives of individuals may shape their works; however, it must be remembered we most often only see a self-projection of the subject. That said, the self-projection can tell us a lot about the author who creates it.

Moreover, Fox explicitly used his own experiences to inform his writing, lending more credence to a reading of his works in light of his life and vice versa. It would not be logical to try and reference all of Fox's works, so I focused on including many of his important firsts along with works supportive to the larger points I make. Essentially, I networked patterns across his work and assessed the way in which these patterns can be understood in light of what we know of his life.

I also use the history of the comics industry and other relevant contexts to inform my readings of both Fox's life and his work. In relation to this, it is worth noting that the concept of ages within the comic industry is largely arbitrary and limiting; however, I find it useful in constructing the narrative of the industry as a whole and these ages serve as a way of contextualizing what Gardner Fox was doing in relation to the larger picture of which he is a part.

This story starts when a friend from grammar school named Vincent Sullivan asked Gardner Fox to write for him at DC Comics. After earning a Bachelor of Arts and a Bachelor of Laws, Fox was admitted to the bar in 1936 and he had been working as a lawyer at the time of Sullivan's offer. According to Fox, he was the first professional writer hired to write comics.[5]

For two years, he wrote comics at night while practicing law during the day. When Maxwell Charles Gaines started *Flash Comics*, he requested Fox pen both of its headlining heroes. Fox gave up practicing law shortly afterward. Still, he was able to use his legal knowledge in his writing and remained a voracious reader.

In 1953, Fox released his first novel, *Borgia Blade*. Fox liked the change of pace; by switching back and forth between comics and novels, he felt he was able to keep his writing fresh. He engaged with other forms of writing as well with letter writing being of special importance as the practice extended to his fan base, which included people who would later go on to become big names in the industry.

Fox would also interact with these fans through fanzines and at comic conventions. As such, Roy Thomas describes him as "one of the 'patron saints' both of *Alter Ego* and early comics fandom" (17).[6] What this biographical information boils down to is that Fox was an intelligent man who found pride in his work as a writer, and knew the power his words had on his fans.

In Part One of this book, I examine the way Gardner Fox's early life and family history helped put him on the path to becoming the kind of writer we know him to be. Fox's writing career started with articles for his high school newspaper and continued through college where he not only wrote articles but also served as editor. This experience would influence how he worked with his editors later in life and taught him the power of the press. His time in college also taught him research methodology, which is exhibited in his many research materials. Of these items, I analyze the scrapbook he built as a means of accurately contextualizing his stories within the short timeframes he was forced to work. This served a dual role as it also permitted Fox to transfer the knowledge he gained to his readers, who he wanted to educate as well as entertain.

In Part Two, I review the start of the comic book industry, and Gardner Fox's role within it. I examine some of the first comic stories he wrote, and the major characters he developed during that time, including Batman, on whom Fox had an early impact on. I also explore some of the characters Gardner Fox co-created, alongside their introductory issues, with an emphasis on Flash and Hawkman. The primary lens through which I frame my analysis of these issues is through Will Brooker's concept of comic book authorship. Gardner Fox's work can be recognized from his use of pulp aesthetics, heavy exposition, and humanitarian themes as well as his focus on justice and insertion of educative factoids. One of the reasons these commonalities are easily included in his work is the fact that many of his heroes are well educated, much like Fox himself. Another facet of his authorship that has biographical meaning is his focus on justice. The comics industry provided him an opportunity to make a living exploring justice in a similar manner as being a lawyer might have provided him. Ever the professional, Gardner Fox developed a strict writing schedule and writing process that I delve into. The birth of his children also gets mentioned because Fox was one of only a few people working on comics who was in the same standing as a growing number of concerned parents who would have a major impact on the industry.

In Part Three, my focus is Gardner Fox's work on the Justice Society of America in conjunction with the criticisms directed at his writing of Wonder Woman as the secretary of said team. Of everything Fox wrote, it is the Justice Society of America that is widely cited as the pinnacle of his career. The formation of this first super-hero team is one of the most important moments in comic book history in addition to it being some of Fox's best and most representative work. Through the team, Fox showcases humanitarian issues surrounding war such as racial and religious hatred, war-orphaned children, and starving civilians. In my examination of these elements, I take World War II propaganda into consideration. I also discuss the way his writing in this era can be understood as a result of his Vincentian beliefs coupled with his inability to physically serve in the US Army. In regard to Wonder Woman, many people describe her secretarial role as particularly sexist. Gardner Fox did write the stories where she was made the secretary; however, there were extenuating circumstances. In order to refute these claims, I cover the reasons that William Marston created Wonder Woman and then cross-compare Fox's unpublished script for a six-page solo adventure featuring her with

the version that was rewritten by Marston. I also include a discussion regarding some of the pre-conceived notions we bring
to these topics and survey other strong female characters Fox
wrote for comparison.

In Part Four, I cover the shift from the Golden Age to the
Silver Age and the range of writing Fox did during this tumultuous time when censorship was brought to the industry. Fox
was one of a few who continued to find writing assignments
during the related slump in sales. This transitional moment
in comic book history was also when Fox wrote his first book-
length story. I explore his historical fiction novel *The Borgia
Blade* as well as the personal responses he garnered from it,
and from his other work. Gardner Fox wrote in a wide variety
of genres at the time, and I emphasize his work in the western
and horror genres in particular. His continued return to the
western genre throughout his career motivated him to purchase and adapt *The Plot Genie: Western Story Formula*, which
elucidates his plotting methodology and common themes. His
horror comics are crucial to delve into given that genre's role
in the arrival of the Comics Code Authority. I detail why this
censorship happened along with the impact it had both on the
industry as a whole and Gardner Fox individually. Specifically,
I track how Fox often dealt with the Comics Code's rules by
taking the supernatural elements in his stories and making
them safe though contextualization.

In Part Five, I look at the return of super-heroes in the
Silver Age. The rise in science fiction's popularity informed
these super-heroes. I analyze this link, and its importance in
the era. I also look at the way in which Fox's explicit humanitarian exhortations return, and compare his handling of
race and disability to his prior efforts. The main location for
these exhortations is the Justice Society of America and the
revived version, retitled as the Justice League of America.
I examine Fox's use of Gardner-Fox-the-character and what
that suggests. This is also when I discuss bigger picture topics
such as the impact of Marvel becoming the rival company we
know it as today along with the trend it kicked off for relevancy, on which Fox places two important caveats: putting
entertainment value at the forefront and making sure the

topics will stay relevant. It was during this era that comics fandom arose, causing a larger number of people to learn of Fox's work around the same time as his work was gaining more general awareness though Batman being on the small screen. The television show also brought Fox the opportunity to write Batgirl. I investigate the ways he used her as an opportunity to write for a female character where her gender is an intended identification point and argue that he used his sister as the main influence for Batgirl. Sadly, things soon take a turn for the worse. I detail the little-talked about Writer's Strike and the stroke Fox suffered following it. It is my argument that this strike forms the end of the Silver Age.

Finally, in Part Six, I focus on Gardner Fox's sword-and-sorcery novels, retirement, and legacy. Sword-and-sorcery was popular, thus allowing Fox to fulfill his childhood dream of creating a hero of his own. He produced several and I compare his two most popular heroes, Kothar and Kyrik, using data mining as well as traditional methods. I also briefly look at his hero named Niall of the Far Travels published in *The Dragon*. This leads to an overview of the board game Fox created, which is important to the narrative of his life in that it brought him to GenCon X, where he met Timothy Truman. This meeting brought Fox back into comics again, providing the opportunity to see how Fox's perspectives had shifted in his final years. All evidence points to these years being joyful and his children proved just as successful as he and his sister were. After his death, I detail some of the many references and tributes to him, including Hawkworld. Finally, I mention other fans who are helping Fox get the acknowledgment he deserves for his accomplishments.

Gardner Fox's biggest claim to fame is as the co-creator of the Flash, who is arguably the fourth pillar of DC. While that continues to be significant, it is diminutive to many of Fox's contributions across the comic industry and beyond. It is my hope that this book will bring these contributions to light. In addition to its entertainment value, I wrote the book so that each chapter can stand on its own for academic work. This feels like something Gardner Fox would have wanted given his educational background, his interest in knowledge for the sake of knowledge, and his enjoyment of the intellectual conversations he had with fans about his work. It can be fairly argued that Fox's writing is formulaic and imitative with a lack of characterization; nevertheless, his works are well-crafted, the quality of writing is solid, and the creativity he regularly exhibited makes up for the skills he lacks. More importantly, his worlds are fun, informative, and often filled with moral lessons. He educated many a reader through these means and raised his children with the same values.

The mild-mannered Gardner Fox lived a mostly uneventful and privileged life. It was through pounding away on his typewriter that he was able to have his daring adventures and make a positive impact on the world around him. He truly is an unsung hero and it is now time to sing his praises.

Timeline

1911, May 20: Gardner Fox is born

1916, May 25: Fox's sister, Catherine (Kay), is born

1929: The Great Depression begins

1932, June 9: Graduated from St. John's College with a B.A.

1936, August 19: Admitted to the Bar

1937, November 14: Married Lynda J. Negrini

1937, May 10: *Detective Comics* #4 is released, which contains Fox's "The Evil Oak"

1938, April 18: The Golden Age of comics begins with *Action Comics* #1

1940, January: *Flash Comics* #1 released , with Fox co-created characters the Flash and Hawkman

1940, April 9: Jeffrey Francis Fox is born

1940, November 22: *All-Star Comics* #3, featuring the Justice Society of America is released

1941, December 7: Pearl Harbor is bombed and America joins World War II

1943, March 21: Lynda Anne Fox is born

1944, September: "Weirds of the Woodcarver," his first short story, appears in *Weird Tales*

1945, September 2: End of World War II

1951, July 25: Gets new agent, August Lenniger

1953: Fox releases his first novel titled *The Borgia Blade*

1954, April 19: Fredric Wertham's *Seduction of the Innocent* is released

1954, October 26: The Comics Code Authority is formed

1956: The Silver Age of comics officially begins with *Showcase* #4

1960, August 25: *Justice League of America* #1 is released

1961: *Alter-Ego* #1 is released

1961: Wins Alley Award for Best Single Issue, *The Flash* #123, "Flash of Two Worlds"

1962: Wins Alley Award for Best Script Writer

1963: Won Alley ward for Favorite Novel "Crisis on Earth One" and "Crisis on Earth Two"in *JLA* #21 and #22

1965: Participates in the first creator panel at the New York Comics Convention

1965: Won Alley for Best Novel "Solomon Grundy Goes on a Rampage" *Showcase* #55

1966, January 12: First episode of *Batman* the television series airs

1967: The Gardner Fox Collection is donated to the University of Oregon

1968: Fox "pushed out" of DC

1971: Honored at the New York Comic Art Convention

1977: Warlocks & Warriors is released through Tactical Studies Rules (TSR)

1978: Received the Inkpot Award at San Diego Comi-Con

1982: Awarded the "Jules Verne Award for Life-time achievement" at Skycon II

1985: Fox made one of the honorees in DC Comics' 50th anniversary Fifty Who Made DC Great

1986, December 24: Fox died at 75

1998: Posthumously awarded a Harvey Award for his career body of work

1998: Entered into the Jack Kirby Hall of Fame

1999: Inducted into the Eisner Award Hall of Fame

2007: Posthumously receives the Bill Finger Award for Excellence in Comic Book Writing

The Fox Family Tree
(Abridged)

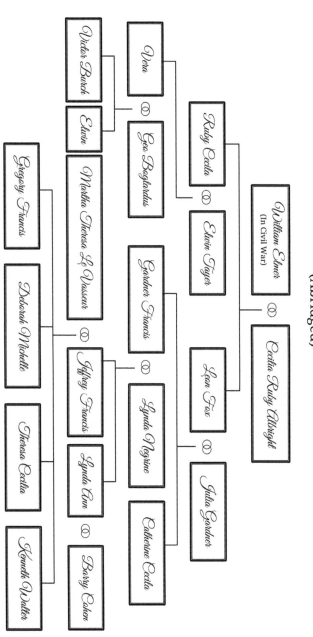

PART ONE

Some day, I promised myself, I would write a hero akin to John Carter or Tarzan or Merritt's Kenton.

—Gardner Fox[1]

CHAPTER ONE

The Youthful Fox

Every story begins at its roots, and the family tree Gardner Fox was born into was enriched with the potential for greatness.

Both sides of the tree had long prestigious branches that exhibited members who rose in position and wealth. These deep roots greatly influenced him. From trying to replicate the actions of his ancestors or writing about them, it is clear that his family history was a large shaping factor on Fox's identity and interests.

His father Leon was perhaps the greatest influence on Fox's perspective. This is made explicit by the way in which his father took control of Fox's education and provided him with a large number of books. Having a family wealthy enough to afford so many books allowed Fox more access to the things he wanted to read when compared to those who had to rely on a library that may or may not be close to their home. Furthermore, the books that he read had a very large impact on the type of writer Fox became.

Despite Fox's dismissal of a privileged lifestyle, he most certainly lived such a privileged life right from the start. These forms of privilege prompted Fox's interests and gave him the ability to follow his passions and share them with the world.

What constitutes the many forms of privilege a person can experience varies greatly. It is easy to say that Fox's life was made easier given that he was a white man who was born into a wealthy family and married a woman of similar status.

How these factors influenced his life were tempered by the many other aspects of his life and the lives of those who came before him. Genealogy was something that several members of the Fox family were interested in and theirs was undoubtably an interesting one to track. The family still has their huge tree framed and mapped out on the wall. There is a real pride in the fact that they were able to trace their lineage all the way back to the ship they took to America.

The first member to make the trip was 15-year-old Richard Fox who arrived on the migration ship *Abigail* in 1635. He was of either Irish or English descent; however, both ethnicities have married into the family making them both Irish and English regardless of this uncertainty. Richard Fox landed in Connecticut and was given land grants in upstate New York. A fair number of Foxes stayed in the area, but a few followed their own path to Salem, Massachusetts, where at least one family member ran into some trouble.

Salem is famous for its witch trials, and having an accused family member perhaps served as inspiration for Fox's use of witches across his work. Before being branded as a witch, his ancestor worked as an innkeeper. When a tenant owed too much back rent, he accused her of witchcraft to avoid paying his debt. Not unsurprisingly for the time, the innkeeper was hanged.

The fact that there was a "witch" in the family may have been one of the things that gave Fox an interest in the supernatural. He purchased a large collection of books from a second-hand bookstore in Manhattan, both fiction and nonfiction, dealing with the subject, and his love of the supernatural pops up in a lot of his writing.

The accusation of witchcraft remained a common storyline throughout his career. More often than not, these witches are a result of intentional or unintentional misidentification. The ones that end up actually being witches are just as humanized as other characters and some even end up as love interests.

The need to prove one's self takes on a much different context in light of the military experience that repeatedly comes up in the Fox family. While Gardner Fox did not serve in the military it was certainly something he idolized.

One very notable soldier was Joel Fox who fought in the Revolutionary War at Lexington and Concord in addition to serving with Washington in the First Continental Army. Even closer to Fox was his grandfather William Elmer, a surgeon in the Civil War. Gardner Fox tried to join the army himself, but his poor eye sight prevented him. Still, this desire to serve was continued through his son, Jeffrey Fox, who joined the army after he graduated from college.

In addition to living vicariously through his son, Gardner Fox was able to join the Sons of the American Revolution and his daughter, Lynda Fox-Cohen, joined the Daughters of the American Revolution. In many ways, she too drew from this rich history to promote the family's past.

While Fox had a plethora of influential people in his family that he latched onto for inspiration, it was his father that made the biggest impact. Described as a stereotypical New Englander, Leon Francis Fox was born on October 15, 1883, in Somerset, New York. Leon was raised in a Quaker home in Rochester, New York, near an orchard the family owned until the late 1990s. A number of his Quaker descendants still live in the Buffalo, New York, area. Even at a young age, he showed upstate moxie by catching and training a wild ferret to help him catch rabbits. He would send the ferret down rabbit holes to chase them toward the exit hole, where he would be waiting with a net. His rural upbringing informed many of his world views. Frugality was important to him and he was much more interested in simpler and practical pleasures such as gardening, hunting, and reading. He passed these traits on to his son and daughter.

Leon's family moved to Niagara Falls before he enrolled at Purdue University. This is especially impressive, as he didn't have a high school diploma. Much like his son, Leon remained active in his university years. Historical records suggest that he formally joined three clubs focused on various different subjects, intimating that for Leon, college was both an academic and social affair. His senior class yearbook, titled the *Purdue Debris*, states that "Foxie" "brings with him an awe-inspiring appetite for the beautiful. He is looking for a telephone job where pole climbing is the chief requisite to a lofty position. With revolver and suit case in hand he often goes out in search of a hair dresser" (103).[2]

The disjunction at work in this description is telling with his more rural side being represented by the inclusion of the revolver in addition to the status he achieved at school, as is seen in his focus on presenting himself well. Leon's interest in fashion and grooming is further supported by the accompanying photograph. Leon's careful attention to self-presentation is something that his son picked up as well.

This ability to look the part is crucial when trying to maneuver oneself upward and, as the yearbook passage stated, he was indeed looking for a lofty position. For Leon, this meant the still fairly innovative technology surrounding telephones. Leon Fox's thesis was titled "A Comparison of the Electric-Magnetic and Electro-Static Disturbances in Telephone Lines." He had a drive to reach high places and being on a telephone pole is one way to do it. In 1906, Leon graduated with a B.S. in Electrical Engineering. At the age of twenty-four, Leon married Julia Veronica Gardner on September 12, 1908.

Julia Gardner's family also held a position of authority in their community. Her father worked as a policeman in Syracuse, New York. Still a point of pride, the family continues to preserve his commemorative retirement billy club. Another heirloom from the Gardner side that family members list when talking about how Gardner Fox was influenced by his heritage is a piece of the battleship *Maine*, which was sent to Julia's family after the death of her brother, Chief Petty Officer Thomas Joseph Gardner.

The *Maine* was best known for its part in starting the Spanish-American War after the "yellow press" blamed the explosion of the ship on Spain. In fact, it's likely that the cause was a fire that ignited from its ammunition stocks.

Julia's daughter, Lynda, also took an interest in her mother's side of the family and felt equally proud to have a great uncle who went down with the *Maine*. Julia was a first- or second-generation Irish Catholic immigrant. Leon converted in order to marry her, an event that would shape Gardner Fox's devotion to Catholicism throughout his life.

Leon Fox's yearbook photo.
(Purdue DeBris Volume XVIII)

The newlyweds were ready to begin the next chapter in their lives. They moved to an affluent neighborhood in Brooklyn and had their first child on May 20, 1911. Passing down Julia's maiden name, he was born Gardner Cooper Fox. Most know him as Gardner Francis Fox, but the name Francis was actually his confirmation name and his father's middle name. This became something of a family tradition, as both Gardner Fox's son and his grandson also carry the middle name of Francis.

Things were looking bright for the young family even though World War I had broken out when little Gardner was just three years old. His parents must not have been too worried because, one year before America joined the war, they gave him a sister named Catherine Cecelia Fox on May 25, 1916.

Fox may not have been fully aware of everything going on during this time in history, but many cultural details from the World War I era found their way into his Justice Society of America work, including women taking up jobs outside of the home, food rationing, and the ubiquity of war propaganda.

Despite the war, Gardner Fox had a happy youth. His family could be described as modestly wealthy. They even had a maid. Fox grew up in a home where attending black-tie affairs and show openings was a normal part of life. Even during the Great Depression, he continued to participate in cultural and social affairs of this sort. With Leon's growing prestige as vice president of engineering for AT&T, the family's status and wealth remained secure.

A high mark in his career was when Leon took part in the transformation of Long Island from mostly backwoods and farmland to the urban landscape we know now, when he was placed in charge of putting up the preliminary phone lines in eastern Long Island. Showing his "appetite for the beautiful," which was mentioned in his yearbook, Leon fell in love with the area and would talk to his son about it.

This level of success allowed a lifestyle many could not afford at the time. Julia Fox thought nothing of serving twelve plates of oysters at a dinner, along with the right wine served from the right glass appropriate for each course. As a full-time housewife, Julia had time to pay attention to these kinds of details. Martha Fox, Gardner's daughter-in-law, described her as a "gorgeous Gibson girl," yet she also claims that there was a certain wildness to her that both Gardner and his daughter shared. She expected to be treated like the lady, and would often order her husband around.[3]

Julia was responsible for most parental duties; however, Leon held strong sway over his children, in particular, their education. This early focus on academic preparation enabled lasting success, for both Gardner and his sister, Kay, became successful students. And despite the fact that their upbringing may have seemed fairly lenient by the standards of the day, they were expected to follow a lot of rules.

According to family legend, their parents used common sayings to enforce desirable behavior. These sayings were still being used by Gardner's son, Jeffrey, albeit delivered in a more playful tone. His children were under the impression that family sayings should always be taken seriously when offered by older generations. Examples of these sayings include: "Spare the rod, spoil the child," "Idle hands are the Devil's playground," and "Children should be seen and not heard."[4] Gardner was known to use the latter as a way to telling his children and grandchildren to read. It's possible that Leon used this same logic because of his interest in his children's education.

Access to books was omnipresent. Indeed, more than any other factor, it was the sheer amount of books that had the biggest impact on Gardner and Kay. For many, having a large number of books was a status symbol at the time, but, for Leon Fox, it was a way to ensure his children's intellectual success. There was one Christmas in the 1920s where he reportedly spent hundreds of dollars on books as a present for young Gardner. According to the Bureau of Labor Statistics's Inflation calculator, $1.00 in 1920 had around the same buying power as $12.77 in 2017.[5] This means that even if he only spent $100 on books as a present, it would be like somebody spending around $1,277 in 2017.

Given the circumstances, it isn't surprising that Gardner became a writer and Kay became a librarian. Gardner was a voracious reader and it was constantly his main interest. He read just about everything with his favorite genres spanning world history and mythology to pulp science fiction and adventure.

Even at a fairly young age, Gardner Fox knew that he wanted to write his own stories. In several letters and interviews he told the same story of when this thought first occurred to him. It was on his tenth or eleventh birthday and the author that prompted it was Edgar Rice Burroughs. Fox's family had moved to Brooklyn in 1925 and he fondly remembers sitting on a brownstone stoop in his neighborhood reading. In this case, he had just gotten *The Gods of Mars* and *The Warlord of Mars*.

The first of these books was especially impactful. He claims that a whole new world was opened up to him that day and he was "forever smitten by the adventure tale of a mighty swordsman set in an alien and unearthly local. It was my first introduction to science fiction and/or fantasy adventure and I came close to yelling in ecstasy"[1] Showing just how impactful this moment was, Fox would later state, "That day, I began to live, really live deep inside me."[6] He began to save up his money to buy every pulp novel and magazine he could get his hands on. He eventually read everything by Burroughs, but he was also a fan of Harold Lamb, Robert E. Howard, Talbot Mundy, and later Edmond Hamilton. Burroughs remained his main influence when it came to science fiction writing, but when it came to fantasy, Abraham Merritt made quite a lasting impact as well. He continues: "I can still see that cover [*Argosy* magazine], of the ship with Kenton staring at it, in my mind's eye."[1]

It was then that he promised himself that he would one day write a hero like those he idolized in his youth. Little did he know that Vincent Sullivan, who was his friend all the way back to second grade, would help him make that dream possible. They attended an all-boys Catholic high school where Fox wrote for the school's newspaper, of which there is a scrapbook containing these and his later college articles. It was this love of writing that Vincent Sullivan remembered when he called on him to write comics years later.

Fox's literary influences made their way into all of his work. He read both pulps and classics. At a basic level, many pulps share genre conventions with chivalric romance,

Gardner Fox at 5 years old.
(Courtesy of Theresa Fox)

which included a hero with a task of some kind who must protect those unable to protect themselves; the existence of misleading appearances; and the discovery of true love.

The pulps changed over time, and Fox continued to draw from their conventions. Drawing from the work of his science fiction/fantasy idols Burroughs and Merritt, for example, Fox incorporated frame stories including autobiographical details as well as characters who yearn for adventure, instantaneous planetary travel, ancient civilizations, parallel worlds, and strong, beautiful women. Most important for this list is Burroughs' take on difference in his Mars trilogy, of which *The Gods of Mars* was a part, featuring John Carter.

A major theme running through this trilogy is that one cannot judge someone based on color, gender, size, or anything else. In these stories, each person is judged only as an individual instead of basing judgement on any groups that the person belongs to. This is a very common theme across Fox's work.

While Fox's writing style remained tied to the pulps, he often drew content from literary classics as well. His knowledge of the classics often takes the form of cultural allusions to well-known legends and narratives. One example of this is in *The Flash*, "Under the Sorcerer's Spell," where the introduction makes an explicit reference to Shakespeare's *Macbeth*: "'Double, double, toil and trouble, fire burn and cauldron bubble.'" One of the witches in *Macbeth* muttered this line hundreds of years ago, but we doubt if she could have cooked up any more trouble than the Flash ran into the day he met Shrimpo the Great."[7]

Fox could have just written a blurb detailing the power of Shrimpo the Great, but he referenced *Macbeth* as a comparison point, going so far as to quote from the play, thus enabling his readers to follow-up should they choose to read more.

Intriguingly, the legend also includes a biblical reference to the Witch of Endor. It is hard to say how much his desire to encourage enculturation and humanitarianism came from the books he was reading or his religious beliefs, but considering that he read them at such a young age, it may be some combination of the two.

This combination is made clear in the way he wrote under his confirmation name. Catholics usually have children go through confirmation around the age of 13, but it could be later. It is when a person must make the decision to commit themselves to the faith and undergo classes that facilitate their initiation into it.

Along with this process is the taking on of a confirmation name drawn from a saint with whom that person identifies with or aspires to emulate. Deciding one's confirmation name is not something that is taken lightly. Saint Francis of Assisi seems to be a strong fit given Fox' interests. The saint was born wealthy, served as a soldier, and gave up his luxuries to live a contemplative life following Jesus's model. It is interesting to note that while he may not have kept " Cooper" in his name for religious reasons, Cooper does make it into many of Fox's pen names.

As is the case with anyone, many factors helped shape Gardner Fox's identity and career path. He was privileged to have such an inspirational family tree on which to draw from, with his father being particularly helpful in shaping Fox's interests. It was his father who provided him the Edgar Rice Burrough books that would set him on his path to create a hero on par with those he read in the pulps. Aspiring high-school writers have a lot of growing to do and his family remained supportive.

By the time Fox arrived in college he had more freedom to study what he wanted to, and his formative loves prompted him to pursue a focus in history and English—two subjects central to the broadening of his cultural understanding of the world, which he regularly brought into his stories as a means of deepening them while also educating his readers.

CHAPTER TWO

Courage in the College Years

Near the start of Gardner Fox's college years, a formative event took place that made it clear to him what profession he wanted to go into. While Fox was guilty of carrying illegal weapons, the justice of the peace understood he harbored no ill intention. The family had recently moved to an incorporated village in Nassau County, New York, named Bellerose. At eighteen years old, Gardner Fox, along with his friend and fellow Bellerose resident Robert Meenan, decided to head out to Heckscher State Park at East Isplip. Unfortunately for the boys, they were carrying two .22-caliber rifles and a 16-gauge shotgun when State Trooper John Healy spotted them. They were arrested and given a court date. On November 30, 1929, the boys pled guilty and Justice of the Peace Arthur G. Griffith fined them $25 each; however, he let them keep the guns, despite the fact that they are ordinarily confiscated in such cases, because the boys claimed ignorance of the law prohibiting guns in state parks.[8]

This act of mercy may have been what helped Fox choose his educational path. It was fair treatment in action, and would have strongly appealed to Gardner Fox's vision of justice, which is at the root of a large amount of his work.

With his path clear, Gardner Fox set out to make himself the best version of himself he could and his college years would provide him with the requisite tools. After the success his father was able to achieve in thanks to his education at Purdue, Leon Fox prioritized education and, unsurprisingly, Gardner followed in his father's footsteps by getting the most he could out of his college years. This is when we see Fox discover his focus on justice, a love of fencing, and the development of strong planning and organizational skills. The double major in English and history he earned before he went on to law school was especially helpful for his writing career and he considered himself to be the first professional writer to join the comics industry.

Fox prioritized a wide range of activities during his college years, suggesting that he saw his time at the Vincentian Catholic St. John's College as an opportunity to expand multiple skills. He served on committees for dances, vigilance, and even one for the chairman cap and gown. Like his sharp-shooting father before him, Fox picked up varsity rifle and joined the basketball, golf, and football teams. He continued to support his college teams by attending St. John's games with his son later on in life. That said, of the all the sports he joined, it was fencing that continued to hold his interest. Fencing was a regular part of his brainstorming sessions. Both Sheldon Mayer and Julius Schwartz report sparring with him long hours into the night while coming up with ideas for whatever comic they were working on. As a sophomore, he earned a minor letter and later became a specialist in saber and joined the varsity team that, without a professional coach or financial backing, turned themselves into one of the most formidable teams in greater New York over the span of just four years.

Somehow, he also found time for dramatics, the student council, the speakers association, and he was secretary of the Sigma Tau literary fraternity. The fraternity was founded in 1929 under the patronage of St. Thomas Aquinas, and the last year of Fox's time there was a high mark for the organization. Members reportedly took part in individual productions to further the study of literature and by occupying important positions in the literary fields of the college.

Fox rose to the position of editor-in-chief of the independent student newspaper, the *Torch*, and also worked as editor of the school year book, the *Vincentian*. All this hard work did pay off as he received recognition through the highest honor the school had to offer.

Initially established in 1928, the Skull and Circle is an honor society regarded as the highest that one could achieve at St. Johns. It is the goal of many incoming students. The review process is long and arduous, including things like academic

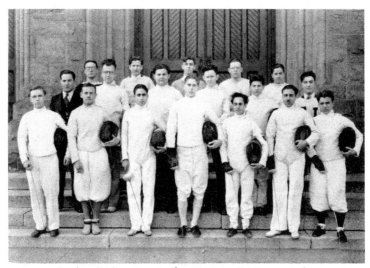

*Gardner Fox's senior year fencing team. Fox is one student
in from the left in the front row. (Vincentian 1932)*

status, participation in social activities, and moral character. Once selected, all the soon-to-be seniors form a semi-circle on the floor of the gym on Tap Day listening for the president to declare who will be "Skull Number One." This is something that is highly desired as it is an announcement to the entire college that not only is the person tapped being recognized for their hard work ,they "may enter the sacred portals of the immortals of St. John's" (96).[9]

On May 7, 1931, Fox was among the group of young men on Tap Day for the class of 1932. They were standing beneath the backboard of the gym in expectant silence waiting for the solemn pronouncements. The senior members of the previous Skull and Circle year marched into the room. As the ceremony started, the primary senior, placing his firm hands on Fox, decreed to the whole college that Fox was "Skull Number One!"

This was the high point of Fox's undergraduate career and it was the main focus of his entry in the yearbook for his senior year. It states: "The day on which Gardner was tapped Skull Number One for Skull and Circle saw the culmination of a college career the activities of which ranged from athlete to editor. Gardner is the only man in the history of the college to edit both

Torch and *Vincentian*,
and the splendid
manner in which he
handled both of these
positions speaks well
for his executive
abilities. Happy days,
Gardner" (47).

While being
tapped Skull Number
One must have been
quite the moment,
the yearbook entry
also points to his
experience with
editing as being a big
part of his college
years. Naturally,
he went on to edit
the February 1932
St. John's College

*Gardner Fox's senior photo for his
yearbook. (Vincentian 1932)*

Alumni News. This work experience must have had quite the
impact on Fox as he maintained very good relationships with
his later editors and was known to unquestionably followed
their instructions.

As if all this were not enough, Fox had one more big surprise
at his undergraduate commencement ceremony. He graduated
from St. John's College with a Bachelor of Arts on Thursday,
June 9, 1932. Even though he was not finished with his
schooling, Gardner walked in the ceremony and, in addition to
being awarded his diploma, he received another award for his
accomplishments. In recognition of his distinctive scholarship,
Fox was awarded the Moore Memorial Medal for the highest
standing in senior religion.[10]

This must have meant a lot to Fox, whose Catholicism was
a significant part of his identity. He never missed attending
mass on Sunday, and prayed every single day of his life. It
was such a big deal that his son Jeffery would tell hyperbolic
stories about being forced to sit in the car for over an hour

during their vacation just to attend some kind of Christian church. His graduation medal was the icing on the cake of a highly successful undergraduate career marked by his commitment to religion and belief.

Continuing his education, Fox went on to earn a master's degree from St. John's School of Law where he experienced further success. Gardner sustained certain activities such as fencing, but he also started to do more planing for his future. He began to attend meetings and dinners that were sure to be the perfect place to build connections and establish himself in that world. The most important professionalizing maneuver he made, though, was joining the prestigious legal fraternity Phi Delta Phi. He was initiated into the international legal fraternity at St. John's School of Law on March 24, 1934.[11] The fraternity focuses on promoting "a higher standard of professional ethics in the law" and is both the second oldest North American legal organization in continuous existence and the largest legal fraternity in existence.[12]

Everything seemed well in order for him to go on to a prosperous legal career. Thankfully, these years also provided him tools that were invaluable to him as a writer.

One of the ways that we can most clearly see Fox's education informing the way he wrote is through the scrapbook that he built. He was a researcher who spent many hours reading through the materials in his extensive collection at home, at the Mount Vernon Public Library, and anywhere else he might come across something interesting. Anything he thought might be useful for his writing, he would carefully preserve in various locations. These included his card catalogue, a highly organized plot book complete with homemade tabs, and a Whitefield composition notebook filled with well-organized citations.

Of these self-created reference books, the scrapbook is the most elucidative. Scrapbooking was something that he had experience in before as is evidenced by the missing scrapbook containing Fox's high school newspaper work.

Additionally, his sister Kay, who was head librarian of the Keene Public Library for twenty-nine years, was the likely creator of the archived scrapbook collecting articles featuring the library and the like.

At the time, scrapbooking was a fairly common practice regardless of gender. They were often used as a way of filtering through the surplus of newsprint and other media at the time in order to follow a trend or track a story. They could also serve as a method of preserving personal and family histories.

As scrapbooking was already an established activity for Fox, it would be natural to apply that methodology to his research practices, too.

The many materials he preserved serves a dual purpose in that they helped him to construct his stories while also showing us who Fox was as an author. When talking about what kinds of scrapbooks different types of people make, Ellen Gruber Garvey, in *Writing with Scissors: American Scrapbooks from the Civil War to the Harlem Renaissance*, singles out authors specifically when she states: "Authors clipped records of their work and made scrapbooks intended for reference, keeping accounts of publications" (10).[13]

The Gardner Fox Collection contains those many examples of Fox's written works as well as business correspondence and the like, therefore making much of the archive supplemental to the scrapbook from this perspective. Fox collected these materials to help him become the best writer he could be. We can look at the clippings he saved as essential to his creative process because of the very fact that he saved them. The wear and tear of the scrapbook is also revealing as it showcases the frequency of use throughout those demanding years. As he read through the many mediums he clipped from, he selected things he found the most inspiring for his writing, thus building his own media source that could have functioned much as the internet does for creators now.

Returning to Ellen Gruber Garvey, she explains that: "Many scrapbooks are diaries of sorts—a form of writing that may or may not be chronological but records and preserves elements of life experience and memory cues" (15).

Fox was a well-educated man, and throughout his career as a writer he makes many academic references that reveal his love of knowledge and these are made possible through the use of his scrapbook. References include everything from current events, literature, mythology, history, and even scientific theories. This kind of biographical information can be incredibly important to understanding a person's scrapbook because it provides a context, thus making the scrapbook more legible.

In looking at the actual content of the scrapbook, it is useful to keep in mind the title Fox gave it: "Local Color." The definition of local color, which he later provides within the scrapbook under the section labeled "writing hints," is something that "can create mood for reader, for character, can help to characterize."[14] Much of the scrapbook is made up of titled pages with many types of paper scraps attached to them. Most of the clippings are taped onto the note pages while others are hole punched and included as if they are additional pages.

Almost all the clippings are pictures of some sort. Potentially useful information is also clipped and saved such as the answers to quizzes titled "How much English do you speak?" and "What's in a name?" both of which test readers' knowledge of English slang. Clippings with historical context such as "Life in a Medieval Castle" are included as well.

Fox got most of his clippings from newspapers, magazines, advertisements, comic strips, and other mediums such as *The Bulletin Presents*. He took these clippings and taped them in layers to the pages in the scrapbook to create something he could flip through when he needed to describe the "local color" he wanted to invoke in the panels he was envisioning.

After this section, there are many handwritten notes, illustrations, and bits of information he might need, all organized by a table of contents. The table of contents includes tables, loot, lingerie, occupations, and superstitions. Within those groupings, many repeated contexts appear such as Western, Viking, Medieval, Oriental, Classical, and Roman. These categories do have some overlap regarding picture type and information type; however, there seems to be no specific relation between the first two sections, organizationally speaking. Lastly, after the written aspect of the scrapbook, yet more clippings are taped onto pages to flip through.

As a whole, the scrapbook exemplifies what makes Fox such an effective writer, what is important to him as a writer, and points to some of the issues that are often brought up in discussions of his work.

Scrapbook page labeled "Oriental" (Coll008_b0031_ f014_001a, Special Collections & University Archives, University of Oregon Libraries, Eugene, Oregon)

Two of the biggest criticism readers might have when reading Fox's work is that he reproduced the racism and sexism that was, unfortunately, common in Golden and Silver Age comic books. His projects are representative of the cultural understandings at work during the time at which he was writing. Comics from these eras, especially from the Golden Age, drew from different forms of racism in a variety of ways. The flattening of race or ethnic difference by a white man, while a common feature of these times, had the effect of diminishing what today many value as a significant part of their identity or cultural connection.

An example of this is his category labeled Oriental. It should be noted that the term was much more commonly used when he was writing and there is a plethora of evidence pointing to his ability to see all people as more or less the same regardless of their ethnicities.

While not a category of its own, one of the most common images within most all the categories were women. In the context of local color, this speaks to the way in which female characters were (and still are) often used to inform our understanding of male heroes and the situations in which they're placed.

There is a possibility that the high number of women in Fox's clippings could have been a result of the exotification of nonwhite women from the locations he was interested in or a reflection of the gaze-based politics exhibited in his resources.

Literary scholarship and women's studies have since developed methods for reading and interpreting the presentation of women's bodies in visual and narrative culture, the depiction of the gaze, and the power of female agency. A large majority of Fox's writing took place before the formal development of these reading strategies. Hence, from our perspective, they seem dated. Still, it's worth noting that within the context of his own cultural moment, Fox's depictions of women display seeds of resistance to dominant modes of viewing women as passive bodies awaiting conquest.

Fox included a lot of women in his stories when compared to his contemporaries. These women prove to be just as intelligent and capable as the men they share storylines with. In fact, the title hero is often put in a situation where they could not save the day without their female partner. While still tied to his generation, Fox exhibits signs of challenging the conventions of his age.

The scrapbook also reveals Fox's love of books and the potential of gaining knowledge from them. Many of the pages in the scrapbook include citations, so he could go back and reread the books he found useful if the information that he wrote down wasn't enough.

Fox's love of books also comes through in many of his comics with a regular motif of saving books from various threats or making reference to specific books. The previously mentioned *Macbeth* quote in "Under the Sorcerer's Spell" is just one example of these kinds of references.

The repeated motif of saving books establishes a value in them that, alongside seemingly random tidbits of information, could have motivated a reader to do research of their own, creating the possibility for Fox to indeed spread his knowledge. This spreading of knowledge was something mentioned in several letters he exchanged with fans, including notables like early comic scholar and "Father of Comic Book Fandom" Jerry Bails and award-winning comic book writer, editor, and overall supporter Roy Thomas, showing us how rewarding it was for both him and his fans.

The scrapbook he created aided his writing process, but it also gives us the chance to catch a glimpse of who Fox was as a creator and as an educative propagator of the next generation.

In 1935, Fox earned his degree from St. John's School of Law, and spent the following year at entry-level jobs. As a law clerk, he would conduct legal analysis, prepare documents, and handle case research. Fox also served as a legal referee at Kings County Supreme Court for the Title Guarantee and Trust Company. As a referee, he presided over civil hearings focusing on real estate cases like foreclosures. He didn't render judgment, but he would have been personally appointed by a judge in the district, making this something to be proud of. It is clear that, even before he was working as a lawyer, his sense of justice was noticed and appreciated.

CHAPTER THREE

The Trials and Triumphs of Adulthood

Thanks to his years in school as well as his time as a law clerk, Gardner Fox was primed and ready for a bright future. More importantly, his sense of justice was strong and he was eager to start putting it into action. He was right on track with his life, having turning 24 years old, when he took the bar exam on August 19, 1936. Of the 1,417 people who attempted the exam that year, he was among the 720 who passed.[15]

While working as a lawyer, Fox was invited to a life-transforming party where he met the woman of his dreams. Ever the romantic, they began courting and eventually married. Their relationship was complex, as described by their grandchildren and daughter, but they stayed together until death did them part. At the very least, they continued to support one another, recognizing their responsibilities and performing family roles that mirrored the values of Fox's childhood home.

Lynda Negrini, Gardner's wife, was a high-society lady who graduated from finishing school. The importance she placed on status may have been difficult for him to deal with at times, but he always talked about her lovingly. The appearance of many stories across his career that feature super-heroes having honest, multi-faceted relationships with assertive and capable women could be a result of his respect and appreciation for her.

Everything was coming up roses, but something just didn't smell right. In the end, Fox didn't feel like he was able to effectively enact the type of justice he wanted to see in the world through his job as a lawyer; however, when his friend from grammar school invited him to write comics, he discovered another way to fulfill his dreams.

Although many people say they hate playing games when dating, one can learn a lot from playing actual games with someone and this was a key factor for Gardner Fox and Lynda Negrini. Gaming was a big part of Gardner Fox's pleasure time and he took it seriously. He was extremely competitive when it came to any game, whether it was as complex as poker, or as simple as slap-jack. While he was happy to teach someone a game, he didn't have much patience for those who refused to learn. This even extended to teaching his grandchildren how to play. He never let them win unless they earned it.

As his grandson Greg Fox states, "He was a gracious winner and a gracious loser, but don't mess up the rules."[4]

Amusingly, his grandchildren did get their revenge on him more than a few times with one particular game: Uno. Because Gardner Fox was color blind, he was at a distinct disadvantage. As the "master of games," he would sit with his grandchildren around the holiday table and play a game he knew he would very likely lose simply because he would misplay the greens and blues. But, just like he taught them, his grandchildren would take no mercy on him. He seemed to enjoy that even more than winning.

While Uno was a regular game with his grandchildren, bridge was a game that was a big part of his marriage. The couple spent many hours playing it together and as members of a few bridge clubs. That said, it was the still fairly new game of Monopoly that served as the basis of the relationship.

Shortly after he was admitted to the bar, a mutual friend threw a party inviting both soon-to-be-lovebirds. They were introduced at the start of the game. Monopoly is a game that requires a good memory, and a lot of strategy can be involved. People who are good at reading other people have a tendency to win, making this a very quick way to get to know someone.

As a part of their courtship, Gardner Fox once again turned to writing, this time, in the form of love poems. These love poems were a constant in their relationship. In fact, with every gift he gave her, Gardner would include a card and write poetry on every one.

Just as we must be careful in over applying knowledge of the author in our analysis of his comics, short stories, and novels, we must also be careful in our analysis of his poetry; however, we know that these are love letters sent from Gardner Fox to Lynda Negrini, so we can assume that the "I" is indeed Gardner and the "you" is Lynda. These poems reveal a lot about what their relationship was like before they were married and living together.

Even though it shows that the poems are by "Gordon" Fox, they do indeed have Gardner's home address at the time on them and the family is certain they were written by him. This could be a typo or could very well be the first time he used a pseudonym. If it was a conscious decision, it would be a protective choice considering his strong Catholic faith and the sensitive material therein

In "Tarry No Longer," we see Gardner Fox asking Lynda to take their relationship to the next level. The poem is made up of short imperative sentences, with the subject as the reader, who in this case is Lynda. It almost sounds as if he is being demanding of her, but he references prior shared dreams showing that this comes from a place of consent. Further, he gives all the agency for the final decision to her. He is asking her to accept him and allow him to share her life with him.

```
TITLE: TARRY NO LONGER  By: GORDON FOX
                             28 Hudson Road
                             Bellerose, L.I.


Come for me !

Do not make me wait

Until the rich fulfillment of our dreams

Comes true.

Take me now !

Make me yours alone -

Let me, too, share that road that must be trod
```

"Tarry No Longer." The image cuts off the final line which reads "With you." (Courtesy of Greg Fox)

In "Last Night" we can learn what falling in love felt like to Gardner Fox and we see that his exhortations had their desired effect:

> Last night I held you in my arms
> And in your naked arms, found Love
> That tore and tugged and stoned my heart
> Until that Love found entrance.
>
> And now my hear is cold with fear
> For Love has come and gone away
> To footfalls as your feet depart!
> When will last night come again?

This poem gives the impression that they had started a physical relationship of some kind, which would be a big deal for the devoutly Catholic Fox. This religious tension appears when he describes love as stoning his heart as if love should be punishing him for his actions. The personification of "Love," signified by both the way it is capable of actions of its own as well as its capitalization, both emphasizes the emotion he is describing and removes it from himself. It is a feeling he didn't have before he found it in her and he appears to have tried to resist those feelings at first.

These poems perfectly describe that moment when a relationship becomes serious, when you want to always be around the person you love because it feels so good and life feels empty and cold every time they leave. With every footstep, the possibility of them simply not coming back begins to set in, making you desperate to be in their presence once again, to feel that love come back and warm you. These letters show Gardner's tenderness and the romantic side of his relationship with Lynda that may not always have been visible to those around them.

Despite the fact that the Great Depression was still going on, the wedding was a lavish affair. Gardner Francis Fox married Lynda Julia Negrini on November 14, 1937. The Negrini family was pleased and even announced the couple's engagement in the *New York Times*. Lynda wore a long-sleeve satin gown with a long train and a tiny bit of ruching near her belly to pull the dress in at the waist. It was a tiny dress that her granddaughter Theresa Fox couldn't even fit in when she was 9 or 10 years old. For being at least 5'8", Lynda was a slim

Married couple. (Courtesy of Greg Fox)

size zero at the time. It fastened in the back with around 30 individual satin buttons. Even more impressive was her five carat diamond ring. Fox saw this extravagance as an investment in their retirement, making the ring a tangible symbol of life-long commitment.

The wedding itself was formal and traditional in a Roman Catholic church. Regardless, Gardner's father Leon became drunk at the event, which led, in turn, to his wife Julia's rising anger in response. Apparently, this was the last time Leon ever became drunk in his life.

After the wedding, Gardner Fox's legal career grew. He was responsible for handling the briefs on appeal for the New York City law firm he worked for and tried cases that the older lawyers didn't want to handle.[16]

By all appearances, he had a bright future as a lawyer ahead of him. He even won some judgments that surprised his older colleagues, and himself. It was a fun and exciting job for Gardner, and he had high aspirations.

This was all very exciting for Lynda as well. In her mind, she had not just married a promising lawyer. She was convinced that he was going to become a Supreme Court justice one day. This was important to her as Lynda Julia Negrini was also from an established family and she was very society minded. The Negrini family immigrated from Italy and her father, Matteo Negrini, owned land in Manhattan. As such, she went to boarding school where she learned etiquette and proper behavior.

While Fox was more of a "salt of the Earth" type, he did believe in presenting himself well and found value in decorum.

Lynda took on her role as housewife with relish. While she was doting on her future children, she could be rather tough on her husband. He was just as tough on her, though. For example, he insisted on breakfast being ready by 7:30 every morning, and dinner at 6 p.m. sharp. By 6:02, he would reportedly start getting a migraine. This likely stemmed from Fox being a very punctual person more than anything else. Dinner was consistently something to look forward to as well.

Lynda was a very good cook. She could make classic Italian dishes as well as traditional American meals. Lasagna, Harvard beets, and Welsh rarebit were some of Gardner's favorites.

Because she saw herself as not just Italian, but high-class Italian, Lynda felt the need to maintain a certain appearance and this included keeping an immaculate house. She was also much more concerned with material items than her husband. While Gardner was tough regarding bridge and mass, Lynda covered just about everything else and, while they had some higher-end items, they consistently lived below their means.

Furthermore, as she was the oldest of four sisters, the extended family often revolved around them. This resulted in her half-jokingly being referred to as the "matriarch." In fact, every Sunday they would have dinner at her mother's house and it was a formal shirt-and-tie affair. Clearly, they took turns wearing the pants in the relationship.

Before the end of the decade, the young couple made a large purchase that remains a beloved family treasure. After Leon Fox fell in love with eastern Long Island, he talked his son into buying a cottage on the Peconic Bay in Mattituck, New York. It was a small house on a bluff with a gorgeous view. From their yard, surrounded by tall oak trees, they could see the bay. They spent all their summers there up until the late 1960s and many family members on both sides would be invited along.

Greg Fox remembers that he never had better sleep than when he slept on that porch. The sounds of the wind blowing

The Fox Family's Mattituck Summer Retreat. (Courtesy of Greg Fox)

through the oaks and the gentle waves of the bay could be heard from the porch, making it an especially relaxing place to visit. Gardner's happy place was surely his little cottage on the bluff. That doesn't mean that he stopped writing during his vacation time. He would often bring his large legal pads down to the beach or take his typewriter outside on the porch.

Fox was living the dream. His family wanted him to make something of himself and he was making progress toward that goal. His college years were filled with successes and accomplishments on top of the two degrees he earned.

During that period he sought other opportunities as well. For example, the editorial work he did for his college's independent student newspaper would make a huge impact on his later life because it influenced the way he would interact with other writers and editors.

Although his childhood love of sports never faded, the time Fox spent on the fencing team was especially important.

As he moved toward his legal career, his life continued to look bright and promising. He managed to meet and marry the girl of his dreams, he passed the bar, and maneuvered himself inside the courtroom. These life experiences helped him in his future writing career because they gave him perspectives that he would not otherwise have.

Everything should have been perfect. Yet, despite these signs of success, something was missing from his life. His shift into the comic world would fill that gap, but it wasn't an immediate revelation or a planned career move. It began with a single event, when Vincent Sullivan invited Fox to write comics for him in 1937.

PART TWO

He could imagine and write about justice in its absolute value. Not the way that we see today, bargaining down whether or not something did or didn't happen. ... Sometimes the police make mistakes, sometimes defendants lie, and sometimes the system fails. In a comic book, everyone agrees on what justice is supposed to look like.

—Theresa Fox[1]

CHAPTER FOUR

Fox's First Steps into the World of Professional Writing

It takes bravery to redirect the course of one's life to follow a dream. Many never feel like it is an option. For Gardner Fox, becoming a writer eventually felt like the only option his heart could make. And who do we have to thank for giving Fox this option? His friend from elementary school, Vincent Sullivan, who followed his own passions into becoming an editor for National Allied Publications. When he needed more writers, he thought of his longtime friend and the rest is history.

This invitation took place in 1937, putting the start of Fox's career before the advent of Superman. The sheer length of his career, which didn't end until 1985, establishes him as an integral part of comic book history.

As much as Fox enjoyed working on comics, he didn't give up his literal day job until later. In the interim, he worked on several smaller characters such as Steve Malone, but also one of the biggest: Batman. He managed to live both lives for a while, but his sense of justice was challenged working as a lawyer. In the end, he realized he couldn't live by his ideals and work as a lawyer at the same time.

Through his writing, he was able to explore what justice truly meant to him. This is something people responded to and he quickly found his first taste of success in the comics industry. It isn't easy to stay fast to one's ideals because it can, and does, make life more challenging, but Fox proved willing to change his whole life to do so. Through his comic writing,

Fox found a perfect platform to explore and share his vision of how the world should be.

While Fox worked toward his law degree, the comic book industry began to look familiar with Vincent Sullivan helping it grow. There is some debate over who kicked it all off, but most people give at least some credit to publisher Maxwell Charles Gaines. In 1933, he essentially cut up a sheet of newsprint strips, put them on magazine sized pages, and put the whole thing out under the name *Funnies on Parade*. He, and a few others, were the pioneers of the industry. Instead of being one or two pages within another publication, comics were now a medium of their own. Dimes were harder to come by during the Great Depression, but children were still buying these reprinted comics in droves. This kind of market demand encouraged the creation of comic books with all-new material in them.

In 1935, writer and publisher Major Malcolm Wheeler-Nicholson released the first ongoing and regularly published comic book containing all-new material titled *New Fun*. Soon, a companion title named *New Comics* followed. These would later be retitled as the more recognizable *More Fun Comics* and *Adventure Comics* under the publishing company National Allied Publications. Vincent Sullivan's drive to get into the comics industry came from his love of the Sunday funnies. He joined the comic book industry as a staff writer and, before long, he became the editor for *New Comics* and then *More Fun*.

There were no real precedents for the job this early on, so he took on a range of tasks from creation to distribution. Sullivan would still run into his friend Gardner Fox occasionally and, when he needed more stories, he remembered how Fox always liked to write.

With the Great Depression going on around him, Gardner Fox felt he could use the extra money and he was excited by the prospect. Still, Fox didn't know what he would be getting himself into. Amusingly, Fox's response to Sullivan's question was to ask, "What are comics?" according to an interview he did with Lou Mougin for *Comics Interview* #9. Sullivan replied that comics are "original illustrated stories, somewhat similar to the comics strips appearing in the form of daily newspapers but published in the form of books."[2]

Fox obviously took him up on the offer after this description and wrote his first story for a comic book in 1937. Written for *Detective Comics* #4, the short prose story was titled "The Evil Oak." Credit is given to Paul Dean, a pen name Sullivan shared with Fox. Much like Fox, Sullivan would also use pseudonyms based off of family names. This marks the first of many professional pen names Fox would use.

The story itself was a two-page crime tale about a puzzling murder and a tree with a mysterious hollow. Fox gives his best Raymond Chandler impersonation, replicating Chandler's overall tone and his overuse of adjectives. While borrowing from the noir genre, the story ends with some poetic justice in that the murderer also dies and the detective is quite happy to leave it at that.

Kicking off his comic career in full, the first comic story Gardner sold was "The Lavalle Case" in *Detective Comics* #18. Coming out in 1938, the story features the now relatively unknown Steve Malone, District Attorney. In a letter he sent to Roy Thomas, Fox explained he based the character on his experience in the law courts.[3]

This familiarity motivated him to create many characters with a legal background, thus keeping to the advice many people give: write what you know. He saw Steve Malone as an alter ego of sorts and this could explain why he didn't include much of an origin in the first story, nor thereafter. The writing for Steve Malone has the feeling of a prose writer trying his hand at comics for the first time.

Still, there is something charming about the educated vocabulary and cleverly placed clues. The repeated motif of a legible newspaper allows the reader to play detective right along with the title character. As was common before the debut of Superman, Malone had no costume, secret identity, or special powers aside from his attentiveness to the police radio and overall intellect. He was also a tough guy capable of throwing punches and, if necessary, shooting to kill. Nevertheless, Malone's main goal was to make sure the antagonists saw a court date.

Steve Malone only lasted a handful of years and is not particularly memorable on his own, but he is an important character in Fox's history because the well-coiffed criminal attorney with a strong sense of right and wrong sets the template he would use for many of the characters he would later create. And a certain character's arrival would herald a new age where these opportunities became prevalent.

With its debut of Superman, *Action Comics* #1 changed the comic industry more than any other single issue. Super-heroes had existed before this point, but Jerry Siegel and Joe Shuster's costumed Superman was the first to put all the pieces together in a way that grabbed the attention of the American people. Superman quickly became a headliner kicking off the Golden Age of comics in 1938. The Golden Age is generally accepted to have run from the time of the Great Depression and the start of America's involvement in World War II, or the late 1930s, to the middle of the 1940s. It was during this age that The comic book industry became the single most popular producer of reading material in the child and young adult demographic.

The rise in popularity was fueled by the new "costumed characters" who rose up after the success of Superman. In this one age, hundreds of super-heroes were created as if by assembly line to try and keep up with consumer demand and a large number of them were on Fox's desk at some point in his career. Also on Fox's desk was a story for *Action Comics* #1 about the boxing commission dealing with a dirty fighter titled "The Light Heavyweight Championship," giving him a minor part of this key moment in comics history.

Another link to Fox is the issue's first appearance of Zatara. Even though he is a mostly forgotten character, Fox soon wrote a number of stories featuring the magician and later produced stories about his daughter Zatanna in the Silver Age of comics.

Where *Action Comics* #1 is a big part of comics history in general, *Action Comics* #2 reveals more glimmers of who Fox would become as a writer. The main story he penned is titled "Zatara the Master Magician and the Haunted Farm." Thanks to Zatara's traditional top hat and tails, this can be considered the first time Fox wrote for a costumed hero.

Comic book magicians were once considered contenders for the most popular type of hero before super-heroes took over. Many of them closely resembled Mandrake the Magician, the star of the Lee Falk's long-running newspaper strip of the same name. Like Mandrake, Zatara is a stage magician and his most distinguishing characteristic is the way he casts spells by pronouncing words backward. In Fox's hands, Zatara became more charming and courteous.

Starting with Zatara's investigation of a haunting, the plot is a pulp-influenced murder mystery complete with the classic tropes such as a woman who goes missing and a detective that gets drugged. The supernatural aspects make many more appearances in Fox's work and so does the playful sense of mischievousness we see in this story. An example of this mischievousness is when Zatara turns invisible to retrieve the police and then suddenly reappears in a shocking manner. This reveals Fox's sense of humor as is seen in his other works such as the Flash.

His prolific tendencies are also showcased in this issue with its inclusion of Fox's Pep Morgan story about a baseball player over-coming his fear after breaking his arm. This early story provides the type of moral lesson for which Fox would later be known.

By 1939, Fox had committed himself to living a dual life as a lawyer and a comic writer. While the latter was financially rewarding, he saw it as an enjoyable hobby that wouldn't last. For the first two years of his comics career, the mild-mannered Fox would spend his days practicing law, knowing he would soon get the chance to step into the shoes of the heroes he authored by night. This frame of mind may be one of the reasons he didn't fight to get credit for so much of his early work.

At the same time, he welcomed this part of his life and began to form new relationships. One such relationship was with the similarly tempered artist Bert Christman. David Armstrong's "In Search of Bert Christman: The Short and Adventurous Life of the Man Who Created 'The Sandman,'" published in *Alter Ego*, reveals that this relationship even resulted in them becoming roommates. Christman entered the comic industry a couple of years before Fox, but this didn't stop him from joining the navy. The two of them struck a mutually beneficial deal.

Armstrong quotes a letter where Christman writes, "Gardner has leased another place, and I shall live with him until I get my orders to Pensacola...and I'm giving Gardner the furniture in exchange for living with him, rent free, until I leave" (23).[4]

Fox had the means to help Christman before he went down for his aviation cadet training and the newlyweds must have been happy to receive the furniture for the home they were building. It is very likely they shared ideas while living together and one likely result of this is a Golden Age character named the Sandman.

There is some mystery around the creation of the original Sandman, but many give Fox credit for a part of it. As a big fan of the pulp hero Jimmie Dale, otherwise known as the Grey Seal, Fox had plenty of material to draw from. And he certainly wrote many stories featuring the character.

Unlike the Sandman most people know from Neil Gaiman's hugely successful series of the same name, this Sandman started out as just a public-spirited citizen running around in a green business suit, cape, wide-brimmed fedora, and gas mask. As per his namesake, he used a gun that emitted sleeping gas to sedate his criminals and sometimes sprinkled a handful of sand over them once they were unconscious as a sort of calling card.

Interestingly, despite his never having committed a crime, the police had Sandman on their wanted list. Even though Christman was the first artist to work on Sandman, the artist most associated with the character is Creig Flessel. A mutual friend of Sullivan, Flessel described Fox as a "good, old-fashioned Catholic" as well as a quiet man and a good writer.[5]

He assumed Fox was a better writer than he was a lawyer. In addition to Sandman, Pep Morgan and Speed Saunders were also written by Fox and illustrated by Flessel.

On top of all that, 1939 proved the year Fox would take on a much more well-known character that allowed him another chance to play with character-based motifs, costumes, and gadgets.

After the success of Superman, many people started taking chances on fledgling companies and heroes hoping to be a part of the next Golden Age success story; nevertheless, DC won when they hit it big, once again, with Batman. Their newest success was kicked off when Vincent Sullivan suggested to artist Bob Kane that he come up with a new costumed hero if he wanted to make more money. After producing a subpar character sketch, Kane invited his writer friend Bill Finger over and the two of them created the Batman we all know and love.

Batman made his first appearance in *Detective Comics* #27, which also had two stories from Fox. As the main writer and co-creator, Bill Finger is responsible for much of what comes to mind when we think of the character, despite the fact that Bob Kane took all the official credit for himself.

While less known, Bob Kane did something similar to Fox.[6] In *The Caped Crusade: Batman and the rise of Nerd Culture*, Glen Weldon explains that Kane secretly hired Fox because Finger "tended to agonize over his stories and let deadlines blow past him" (22). Other accounts suggest that it was the DC editor who hired Fox to write a couple of early Batman scripts.

As troubling as this might sound, no animosity arose between the two writers and Bill Finger stayed one of a few people Fox communicated with after they were no longer working for DC. Fox wasn't a firebrand, but he was one of Finger's early advocates.

One example is in *Batmania* #22, where Richard Morrissey asked if Fox wrote some of the early Batman stories and he responded not only by saying he was the first writer "assigned" to the character but also by reminding Rich Morrissey that Bill Finger "had a lot to do with" Batman's first story regardless of Bob Kane's assertions.[7]

The two writers each brought something different to the character with Fox adding in gothic flourishes, more gadgets, and a vigilante attitude.

Fox gave Batman several important key features and set the darker tone many would later replicate. His impact on the Batman mythos isn't as well known, but he scribed more than one might expect in these still formative issues, including a run starting with the third appearance of Batman in *Detective Comics* #29 all the way to issue #34. The first and second issues he wrote contained Fox's first attempt at giving Batman an arch criminal: Karl Hellfern, otherwise known as Doctor Death.

Also in this run was the introduction of a secret laboratory in Wayne Manor where Batman developed Fox's other contributions to the character including his utility belt, complete with gas pellets, as well as wearable suction cups and the famous Batarang.

Similarly, he gave Batman the precursor to the Batplane: the Batgyro. He was inspired by Igor Sikorsky's first successful helicopter flight, marking an instance of Fox using his daily newspaper reading as a jumping off point for his comic writing. The Batgyro looked like a giant bat with a big rotor on top complete with a rope ladder Batman could climb up and down. This became an important addition when Fox took the character to international lands.

In issues #31 and #32, Batman goes on a two-part adventure to Hungary in order to fight a vampire monk who can turn into a wolf. The story invokes Bram Stoker's Dracula with its religious overtones, gothic scenery, and hypnotized women eager to do the vampire's bidding. Unfortunately for Batman, one of these women is his fiancée Julie Madison, Batman's first romantic interest.

This inclusion of a female companion would soon become a characteristic choice for Fox. Unlike the female companions he gave other characters, Julie Madison didn't know Bruce Wayne is Batman. Setting the template for most of his future relationships, she thinks that Bruce Wayne is a lazy socialite, whereas the intriguing Batman is an ideal man.

The story ends when Batman shoots the evil monk with a silver bullet which Stoker did say would kill a vampire. While it might seem out of character for Batman to do this now, his rule against the use of guns had not yet been established.

Long before the Comics Code Authority, Fox had to learn how to write under the DC house code which had a similar set of restrictions. The version of Batman he brought to life may have been quite comfortable telling the bad guys he would kill them if they didn't give him the information he needed in *Detective Comics* #29, his first issue writing for the character, but Bill Finger also wrote an edgier gun-using Batman at the time.

Still, Fox's vampire-focused two-parter ending with Batman killing the monk by shooting him in his coffin was seen as controversial at the time. In *DC Comics: A Celebration of the Worlds*

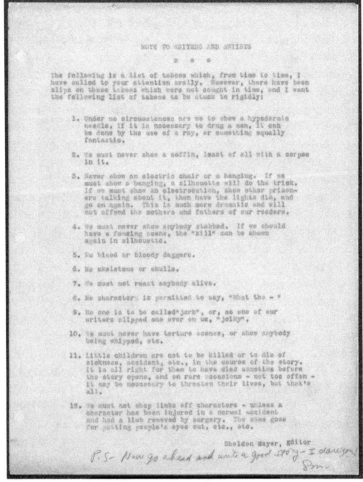

NOTE TO WRITERS AND ARTISTS

The following is a list of taboos which, from time to time, I have called to your attention orally. However, there have been slips on these taboos which were not caught in time, and I want the following list of taboos to be stuck to rigidly:

1. Under no circumstances are we to show a hypodermic needle. If it is necessary to drug a man, it can be done by the use of a ray, or something equally fantastic.

2. We must never show a coffin, least of all with a corpse in it.

3. Never show an electric chair or a hanging. If we must show a hanging, a silhouette will do the trick. If we must show an electrocution, show other prisoners talking about it, then have the lights dim, and go on again. This is much more dramatic and will not offend the mothers and fathers of our readers.

4. We must never show anybody stabbed. If we should have a fencing scene, the "kill" can be shown again in silhouette.

5. No blood or bloody daggers.

6. No skeletons or skulls.

7. We must not roast anybody alive.

8. No character is permitted to say, "What the - "

9. No one is to be called "jerk", or, as one of our writers slipped one over on us, "jelky".

10. We must never have torture scenes, or show anybody being whipped, etc.

11. Little children are not to be killed or to die of sickness, accident, etc., in the course of the story. It is all right for them to have died sometimes before the story opens, and on rare occasions - not too often - it may be necessary to threaten their lives, but that's all.

12. We must not chop limbs off characters - unless a character has been injured in a normal accident and had a limb removed by surgery. The same goes for putting people's eyes out, etc., etc.

Sheldon Mayer, Editor

P.S- Now go ahead and write a good story - I dare you

Memo (Coll008_b0032_f011_001a, Special Collections & University Archives, University of Oregon Libraries, Eugene, Oregon)

Favorite Comic Book Heroes, Les Daniel explains that editor Whitney Ellsworth said the guns had to be removed due to the sense of responsibility DC was beginning to feel for its children readers.[9]

With comics suddenly becoming the most popular reading material for children, there were already concerns about comics in the 1940s and, in an attempt to assuage this, DC tried to impress upon the anxious parents that their stalwart heroes were desirable role models. Part of this consisted of DC's decision to always leave its villains alive at the end of the story. These factors began DC's reputation as being more conservative than other publishers. This desire to appease also prompted editor Sheldon Mayer to send out a list of taboos including dismemberment, corpses, stabbings, blood, skeletons, and cursing. It is likely Fox was one of the people that Mayer states he had already talked to because Fox's Batman stories were not the only ones in which these taboos appeared.

As previously stated, Fox's first attempt at writing Zatara, in "Haunted Farm," has a villain who dopes the hero by sticking a hypodermic needle in his arm. Sheldon Mayer seemed to have a sense of humor regarding this cracking down as he added, "P.S. Now go ahead and write a good story—I dare you!" in pencil at the bottom of Fox's copy found in the Gardner Fox Collection.[10]

Of course, that wasn't a problem for Fox. He did occasionally sneak things in and his work outside the company remained unchanged. Still, Fox always listened to his editors' requests and he greatly decreased his use of these so-called taboos.

More than anything, 1939 was a year of metamorphosis for the still-growing Gardner Fox, and one of the major initiators of this transformation was Maxwell Charles (M.C.) Gaines, who started *Flash Comics*. Either he or his editor, Sheldon Mayer, asked Fox to come up with its two headlining characters.

Created with artist Harry Lampert, inspiration for the Flash first came from Fox's sports days when his coaches would tell him to get things done "like a flash."[11] We get a sense of this in the first issue when the high school football coach is calling soon-to-be-Flash, Jay Garrick a "leadfoot."[12] It should be noted that the idea of having feet of lead was understood as making one slower instead of faster. When thinking of a speedy character, Fox went right to the Roman god Mercury and this can be seen in the winged shoes and helmet the original Flash wore. It is these kinds of design contributions that caused Lampert to give full creative credit to Fox.

Coming up with Hawkman proved a bit more difficult. According to a story he told during his granddaughter Theresa Fox's third-grade Grandparent's Day celebration, he came up with the idea for Hawkman when he was sitting at the window trying to figure out a hero to pair with the Flash. As he watched a bird swoop down and grab a twig, he thought about how the bird could be a lawman and the twig could be a criminal. This school event proved to be the first time Theresa Fox understood just how special her grandfather's occupation was.

When thinking of how to bring in the hawk-like elements, Fox and artist Dennis Neville turned to Egyptian mythology with its human-animal hybrid deities. The original Hawkman was the reincarnation of the ancient Egyptian prince Khufu named Carter Hall. Although the costume gives him the appearance of an Egyptian god, Carter Hall is simply a human who discovers ninth metal, which gives him the ability to negate the effects of gravity. He wears the wings to control his flight and the hawk mask to obscure his identity.

One of the most significant things about the character is his relationship with Shiera Sanders, Hawkman's future wife and a soon-to-be super-hero in her own right. While Fox had already given Batman, Flash, and even Sandman romantic partners, Hawkman's relationship with the future Hawkgirl was an important part of the mythos from the very first issue. In fact, he is one of only a few heroes who had an established romantic relationship right from the beginning.

Starting with the title character, DC's first speedster is one of the most important super-heroes in comic book history, and the co-creation of the Flash gave Fox the opportunity to stretch his creative muscles.

By this time, Fox had some experience under his belt. In the 15-page origin, we get a sense of who Jay Garrick is, how he turns into the Flash, and why he decides to become a super-hero. We even meet his eventual wife, Joan Williams, and her scientist father. The fact that Joan is seen as an equal, graduating from Midwestern University right alongside Garrick, with each of them having academic goals in mind, serves as an early example of Fox's more progressive views.[13]

The story essentially works in two parts with the first half focusing on Jay getting his powers after accidentally inhaling hard water fumes, which miraculously gives him the ability run at super-human speed. The Flash had a different feel when compared to many super-heroes at the time because he was essentially a nerd with a crush who wished he was a football star.

This modest origin shifts when we get to the second part of the story where we see Garrick reading a newspaper, which mentions that some racketeers were able to elude the district attorney's men. He takes action on the grounds that he knows he is fast enough to actually make a difference.

This desire for legal justice is another one of the primary differences between Jay Garrick and other super-heroes. Instead of simply beating criminals up, he will often find ways to gather incriminating evidence or try to force a confession out of a villain. This is perhaps why he was more likely to fight robbers, thieves, and gangsters rather than super-villan groups like the Faultless Four seen in the first issue. While besting these types of villains would be easy with Garrick's speed, he preferred to wear them down until they were willing to confess to their crimes and turn themselves in. This would ensure the villain would receive appropriate punishment instead of having to go through the court system that Fox personally knew might fail.

His favorite method to ensure these confessions was to vibrate fast enough to appear invisible, thereby allowing him to mess with the minds of his foes through what would seem to be a haunting or their guilty conscience suddenly gaining a voice. This also creates the space for Fox's humorous streak to shine. The inclusion of the Three Dimwits, who were loosely based off of the Three Stooges, further emphasized this humor.

Of all of the characters Fox had a hand in creating, the Flash is the most widely known and serves as a cornerstone of DC. Additionally, the Flash is representative of who Fox was as an author.

The concept of authorship within comics is slightly different from its use in relation to other forms of literature, and Gardner Fox's was already visible.

Before the early 1960s, it was not common practice to attach the names of the various creators to their works. This made it necessary to find ways to stand out as authors. In "Fandom and Authorship," Will Brooker provides a definition of comic authorship as "an individual who, whatever his role in the creative process, contributes a recognizable, personal style" (64).[14] In this context, an author's development of a unique style is crucial to developing a fan base so that future work can be ensured.

In the case of Gardner Fox, his work can most easily be recognized through his use of pulp aesthetics, heavy exposition, and humanitarian themes as well as his focus on justice and his insertion of educative moments.

Looking at *Flash Comics* #1, we can already see these things for which he would come to be known. When Fox explains how Flash can safely catch a bullet, we can see an example of the kind of educational information he inserts: "When two bodies travel along together at equal speed even tho they meet, there is absolutely no friction—and therefore no injury!!!"[12]

Similarly, Fox's love of books is on display as is shown by the first time Garrick uses his powers. Instead of rushing to save somebody, he speeds off to get a book from the library for Joan.

These authorial indicators did indeed catch the eye of his readers, who Brooker describes as being put in the position of detectives deducing who should receive the credit for the stories they love. This game-like interaction is shown in the Gardner Fox Collection through the many letters asking Fox if various works were his because they seemed like his other work.

While not as popular as the Flash, Hawkman has a particularly dedicated fan base, making him stand out among the other characters that Fox had a hand in creating. At this point in his convoluted storyline, Hawkman was simply a wealthy research scientist named Carter Hall, who happens to collect ancient weapons. Setting up what is essentially another two-part origin, the story starts when Hall touches a sacrificial Egyptian glass knife and quickly falls into a dream state where we learn about his past life. In this particular life, he was Prince Kufu, who was Shiera's beloved and the enemy of Hath-Set. His dream ends when Hath-Set kills Kufu; however, before he breathes his last breath, Kufu utters his "dying prophecy" that they would live again and one day he would be the victor. Within hours of having this dream, he meets Sheira, who conveniently has the same name, and accepts his story on the grounds that she has had matching dreams. Hath-Set had also been reincarnated, prompting the action of the story. Hall's collection of ancient weapons is a key aspect of the character and often the weapon he chooses reflects the theme of the issue.

More than any other character, Hawkman gave Fox a chance to use his vast knowledge of history and geography. It also gave him a chance to include educative factoids regarding folklore and mythology, which became common in much of his work. The Hawkman origin is even more fascinating as a piece of the Fox canon considering the errors he makes.

Repeatedly, Fox states that Anubis is a hawk god, which is incorrect. The Egyptian god Anubis has the head of a jackal, not a hawk; it's Horus who sports a hawk's head. Fox must have been rushed or he wouldn't have made this mistake. There is also a disjunction in the plot as Hall has no memory of his past life, yet he assembled his costume in 'grim jest' because he 'must have known this night would come.'[15] Designing his costume in the style of the supposed hawk god makes no sense if he had no prior memories of his life in Egypt.

Not only did Fox write the first appearances of the Flash and Hawkman, he also composed a Cliff Cornwall story titled "The Disappearing Plane" and a prose story titled "Warfare In Space (Part One)" all for this introductory issue. It must also be remembered that he was still working full time as a lawyer and doing all this work as a pastime. That would soon change.

For the first two years that Fox produced comic book stories, he continued to practice law and while he described working as a lawyer both fun and exciting, something just didn't feel right. Lawyers weren't getting rich during the Great Depression and M.C. Gaines provided him an out when he started the mostly Fox-helmed *Flash Comics*. According to Fox, he felt he could no longer carry both jobs and simply chose comics over the law. Sheldon Mayer offered a more compelling reason behind this life-changing decision. In *Amazing World of DC Comics #5: Sheldon Mayer The Man Behind the Golden Age,* Mayer describes Fox as being "too gentle a guy" to be a successful lawyer.[16]

According to Mayer, Fox's career as a lawyer ended when, in the middle of court, he realized his client was simply wrong and the other side was right. He said as much out loud in the midst of the trial. If this anecdote is true, it is clear that Fox's sense of justice prevailed over his sense of duty to the legal system. With Fox's strong sense of justice, coupled with his kindness and gentility, it is easy to see how writing was a better option for him. Tellingly, Fox would describe his work in the comics industry as wish fulfillment because his heroes could benefit the world in a way he could not. Regardless of what his actual motivations were when he made such a huge decision, his life changed for the better and he never regretted it.

The comic industry took off in the 1930s and Fox's friend Vincent Sullivan was right in the thick of it. When Sullivan needed more writers, he called on his old friend and subsequently revitalized Fox's creative life. Fox drafted his first story for a comic book in 1937 and just kept writing. He went on to write for minor characters like Speed Saunders before moving on to more well-known characters such as the burgeoning Batman.

One of the ways Fox made this transition was by writing what he knew. This resulted in many of his early characters having common characteristics not just with each other, but with Fox himself. The inclusion of lawyers in his fiction continued to appear throughout his writing career because of his familiarity with their backgrounds. Steve Malone is the most obvious comparison point, but Carter Hall, Cliff Cornwall, and others he had a hand in creating were all handsome, well-educated men with refined taste and a strong sense of justice. This commonality made it easy for Fox to seamlessly insert certain aspects of his authorial signature such as the ever-present educative exposition; intellectual characters are much more likely to give a long and accurate lecture.

Another key part of his signature is the theme of justice and this passion influenced the course of Fox's life more than any other. The comics industry provided him the means through which he could make a living exploring justice in a way that being a lawyer did not.

Fox had already gone from being a promising lawyer who happened to enjoy writing comics on the side to the head writer for the popular *Flash Comics* and his new career had just started.

CHAPTER FIVE

The Official Beginning of Fox's Comics Career

After Gardner Fox quit the law to become a freelance comic writer, he threw himself into his writing and worked hard at improving it. Part of this was working closely with his editors. It was standard practice at DC for the writers to work hand-in-hand with the editors as they plotted. This ensured the stories were always unique and lacked any major plot holes. Fox would invite his editors to work with him in his home and the time spent during these sessions enabled friendships to grow. Working from home also kept his wife involved in their new lifestyle and this family involvement continued when they had children. He also formed a much stronger relationship with Vincent Sullivan during this time and when Sullivan started working for the comic company Columbia, he once again brought Fox on board.

This marks what is likely the first time Fox worked outside of the companies that would one day become DC. Many people within the comic industry technically worked freelance and Fox would go on to write for many more companies.

As to be expected, day-to-day life changed in big ways after Gardner Fox dedicated himself to being a comic book writer and, because these changes occurred at the same time as he became a family man, Fox had to learn how to balance his new life. Gardner and Lynda Fox quickly adapted even though it was not what they originally envisioned for themselves.

On April 13, 1940, Vincent Sullivan married Mary Christine Patrick and Fox attended Sullivan's bachelor party dinner, which also had Zatara artist Fred Guardineer and Sandman artist Creig Flessel in attendance. Shortly afterward, the newlyweds got an apartment in the middle-class neighbor-hood of Hollis Queens at the same time as Gardner and Lynda.

While Sullivan and Fox already had an established friend-ship, their wives too began to grow into best friends. They formed a happy little group. This was well-timed because Fox's parents and sister had also moved. They headed down to New Hampshire to visit his sister Kay. She suffered from a lung con-dition and Brooklyn was not dry, or clean, enough for her health.

As exciting as this must have been, Fox took his new career seriously and built strict schedules around his writing. More than that, he expected others to treat it just as seriously. Unfortunately, because he worked from home, some people wrongly assumed he was willing and able to take breaks when-ever he wanted to throughout the day. This was simply not the way he operated. Indeed, he couldn't have done so while maintaining the high level of work he did, as is shown by his schedule. He worked steadily from 8:00 to 12:00, when he would have lunch, and then go back to pounding away on his keyboard until dinner, which was served promptly at 6:00.

This misunderstanding did occasionally cause some issues to come up between him and the people around him. Once, during the early 1970s, John Fogarty, Fox's nephew, hitchhiked up to Yonkers from Johns Hopkins during spring break. He then walked five miles across town to visit his Aunt Lynda and Uncle Gardner. He unknowingly picked a bad time; Lynda was out when he arrived. This meant Gardner had to stop writing to go answer the front door. He was reportedly so angry about being disturbed while at work that he closed the door in poor Fogarty's face, forcing him to find his way all the way back to where he was staying with his other aunt clear across town.

Fox's comic-writing method was just as detailed and precise. It would start with meeting his editor to establish the plot points needed for whatever story he was working on. Once his task was set, he would sit down in his office with his long yellow legal pads and an ever-present iced coffee to write up the synopsis, including panel-by-panel descriptions of what the illustrators would need to draw as well as narration and character dialog. His scrapbook would have been helpful in determining what contextualizing details to include.

Gardner Fox's Writing Schedule for November and December of 1945 (Coll008_b0032_f012_002a, Special Collections & University Archives, University of Oregon Libraries, Eugene, Oregon)

This is not always as easy as it sounds. At the very first creators panel at a comics convention in 1965, Fox told a funny story in regards to a question about the details included in panels. He explained that, in 1941 or so, he was looking at the artwork for a story he had written and spotted a drawing of an archer on a roof firing an arrow down toward the street. He asked Sheldon Mayer what the archer was doing there because

that wasn't in his descriptions and the editor responded that
Fox had written "Shoot from the roof!" (25).[17] The artist had
misinterpreted Fox's screenplay-style directions for a description of the picture to be drawn.

Once he had a completed synopsis, he would turn it in to
the editors who would would check things, revise any problems
with a synopsis, and finally turn it into a script. Should a synopsis be rejected for some reason, Fox would start the revision
process or begin anew. He took everything his editors requested
very seriously.

While creating a work schedule was helpful, Fox also knew
being a writer meant honing his craft. It can be difficult to
accept criticism, but Fox saved many pages of critiques and
suggestions he received from his editors. Not only that, he
would annotate them with checks and underlines. There are
also several items from "Laurence R. D'Orsay Author and Critic
'Builder of Literary Careers Since 1919'" found in the Gardner
Fox Collection. D'Orsay was an author of many instructional
books for writers in the 1920s and 1930s. Included in the collection is an advertisement for plot cards where he checked
"making your characters live," "write as you feel," and "the
'novel twist' in stories." I was unable to locate those items, but
"Working up Plots From Newspaper Items" was included in the
collection.[18] Current events were often featured in his stories,
proving that Fox did use this strategy.

Even though he was a well-educated man, who already saw
himself as a professional writer, Fox wanted to do his best.
One person who saw this journey all the way from its earliest
stages is Vincent Sullivan. In fact, since that original offer, Fox
had ended up writing for almost all of Sullivan's titles regardless of the company of which he was a part.

While most people know Gardner Fox as one of the people
who helped make DC into what it is today, he also did work for
many other companies, and working at Columbia allowed him
to add yet another character to the list of those he had a hand
in creating. Vincent Sullivan grew to dislike the way publishers
Harry Donenfeld and Jack Liebowitz did business, so he left
National and moved to Columbia Comics Corporation in 1940.
It is through this company that McNaught Newspaper Syndicate

published comic books featuring reprints as well as original features. As part of the move, Sullivan brought Fox on as a writer, along with a few others, including artist Creig Flessel.

Columbia is most famous for its anthology series titled *Big Shot Comics*, which featured its two biggest super-heroes: Skyman and the Face. Fox, as Paul Dean, wrote for both characters. Furthermore, he co-created Skyman with artist Ogden Whitney. The character demonstrated enough popularity to earn his own title, in 1941, and appeared in almost every issue of *Big Shot Comics*.

The Skyman origin feels almost like an amalgamation of Fox's Flash origin with a touch of Finger's Batman origin.

Allen Turner is orphaned due to faulty materials in his father's plane. He grows up with his rich uncle Peter who encourages him to get a university education and live simply. He goes on to become a great research scientist who wants to use his "powers" to prevent crime the way a police officer does. Showing his use of personal experience as source material, Fox also makes Allen Turner a great all-around athlete, scholar, and a man of the finest character. He even has Skyman do some fencing near the end of his first stand-alone issue. Like Batman, Skyman takes on the familiar ruse of a wealthy loafer while he secretly fights crime.

The series includes a Julie Madison-like romantic interest who dislikes Turner for his playboy guise; however, detective Fawn Carroll stands out from that type of character because she is a working girl. This appeals to Turner because he believes working girls are "democratic," meaning that he likes women who aren't snobbish and he values social equality.[19] She also shows the gumption of Shiera Sanders. Columbia had a very small line and only lasted a few years, but Skyman is a rather enjoyable series and the character stands out from the other aviator heroes of the day.

An even bigger super-hero who came out during this time is the H.P. Lovecraft-inspired Doctor Fate, whom Fox co-created with artist Howard Sherman. One of Fox's favorite characters, he is yet another dapper, educated man with a strong sense of justice. What sets him apart are his distinctly Lovecrafian aesthetics.

Lovecraft's stories often postulated an infinite universe that is both completely indifferent to humans and whose unspeakable horrors are just out of sight. If humans came in contact with this cosmic universe, it would drive them insane and leave them utterly defeated.

Despite his interactions with this thematic backdrop, Doctor Fate counters this cosmicism as he is clearly on the side of good and his villains are all inherently evil, as opposed to Lovecraft's more abstract concepts that are beyond such a simple categorization. Doctor Fate is also quite capable of making an impact on the forces around him. Still, this homage is apparent in other places in the text, such as the way Doctor Fate's mentor is an alien who was once worshipped as a god. Doctor Fate also doesn't believe in more traditional monsters like werewolves and vampires, thus mirroring Lovecraft's general distain of them.

Perhaps one of the stories most explicitly influenced by Lovecraft is "Dr. Fate and the Fish-Men of Nyarl-Amen," which features a lost undersea civilization complete with an army of fishmen who once cruelly ruled the world. This tale echoes Lovecraft's classic short story "The Shadow over Innsmouth."

Hidden races, arcane books, and archaic languages make their way into many of Fox's stories. The pulp-loving Fox actually had a connection to Lovecraft in that his future editor, Julius Schwartz, had briefly represented Lovecraft as a science-fiction agent and would later sell some of Fox's pulp work, too.

While Doctor Fate is important to Gardner Fox's career, the character is also important as he very well might have been the first taste of Lovecraft many people ever got.

While Fox's appreciation of Lovecraftian horror served as the primary influence in his co-creation of Doctor Fate, the character still fits many patterns already established in Fox's other creations. For his debut in *More Fun Comics* #55, Fox plays up the mysteriousness of the character by having him appear in a "coal black cloud" after having only been named, thus marking a departure from Fox's previous origin stories as well as keeping it tied to his inspiration. The issue allows Fox to literally ask the question, "Who is Doctor Fate?"[20]

The most distinctive aspect of Doctor Fate is the golden mask covering his full face. Jerry Bails once commented that many of Fox's characters have a "thing on his head" and this particular "thing" is a memorable example.[21] Secret identities were something Fox seemed to be fascinated with, and the Fox-sketched mask hides Doctor Fate's identity so thoroughly that it wasn't clear he was even fully human in his first appearances.

Nevertheless, we do get introduced to the two main supporting characters including his girlfriend, and frequent pants wearer, Inza Cramer along with his main villain, Wotan. Both of these characters fit the Fox mold, with Wotan being a nod to Norse mythology and Inza being an aware participant in Doctor Fate's adventures. Her active positioning in the series is made clear starting in the first issue when she takes on the hero's strength to overpower some evil gorillas.

Along with super-strength, Doctor Fate has a wide range of powers including flight, telekinesis, telepathy, pyrokinesis, and general invulnerability. These all somehow stem from his ability to turn matter into energy and energy into matter through his mastery of ancient mysteries, which apparently includes both alchemy and physics.

There is indeed a human named Kent Nelson under that mask and the "Doctor" part of his name serves as a reminder to the readers that this is a man who has earned these abilities through his educational efforts.

The editor for this issue was Whitney Ellsworth himself, but Fox would much more regularly work with Sheldon Mayer, editor of the DC-affiliated *All-American* comics line.

Flash Comics editor Sheldon Mayer was a regular visitor to the Fox home. While Gardner would sometimes go down to the All-American group's office on Lafayette Street in New York City to plot out a story with Mayer, Anthony Tollin explains in "Origins of the Golden Age: Sheldon Mayer," the editor would most often go over to Fox's house, especially to plot out the issue-length bimonthly *All-Star Comics*, which featured the Justice Society of America. Lynda Fox would make dinner and, after they finished, Gardner would hand Mayer a fencing foil. Their ideas would quickly start flowing as they walked around swinging the foils. Gardner would eventually sit at the typewriter and "throw out an idea...or catch one of [Mayer's]...and [they]'d turn out enormous amounts of material that couldn't have been turned out any other way" (6).[22] Lynda would keep the coffee brewing and they would have a full book-length synopsis before Mayer would leave for the night.

The men grew close and Sheldon Mayer described Fox as a professional, and a fast one at that; Fox is described as being one of a few guys who could just sit down and make a writing decision, or accept one, and then write it without trying to second-guess everything. Mayer also stated that he was "good at running with the ball, and passing it back to you."

Some of this desire for speedy decision-making must have been related to Fox's desire to keep money coming in. Fox only got paid about a dollar a page when he first started out in the 1930s, which wasn't abnormal in the Golden Age. Thankfully, his page rate rose to about three dollars a page during this time. While this is a decent raise, it was still not much to plan a comfortable living around, so Fox had to write a lot in order to maintain his lifestyle. He also paid Lynda to do a fair amount of typing when it got to the revisions stage. This employment was a way he could take care of her should something happen to him because it would allow her to receive social security. More importantly, it involved her in his new life and showed that he trusted her secretarial skills. To use his own word, they were democratic.

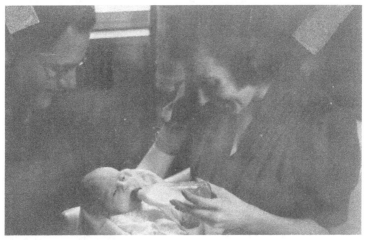

Gardner and Lynda Fox with their young son
Jeffrey Fox. (Courtesy of Theresa Fox)

Three years into their marriage, Gardner and Lynda decided to start a family. Neither of them wanted a large family, but Lynda had especially strong feelings about this. She could even be disparaging of large families, which perhaps didn't fit her ideals of what a proper high-society family should look like. This could also point to the potential struggles she may have faced having three younger sisters.

Jeffrey Francis Fox was born on April 9, 1940, and they were both happy to have a son. Gardner and his son would grow to be quite close and they shared a lot together including an appreciation of sports, education, and silly songs.

Two years later, Lynda became pregnant with the second of their two planned kids. Named after her mother, Lynda Ann Fox was born in Westchester on March 21, 1943. The couple was happy when a little girl arrived because they wanted both a boy and a girl. Gardner adored his daughter and would often come to her defense, such as the time she walked through a Wanamaker's, one of the first department stores in America, and knocked over all of the gumball machines.

It seems as though having a daughter brought out some of Lynda's insecurities because she wanted her daughter to marry somebody with money, thus ensuring she would

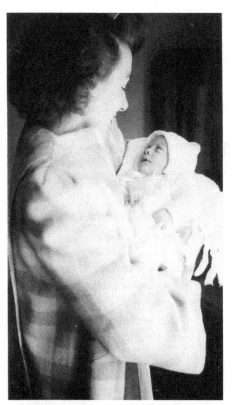

The elder Lynda Fox with her daughter Lynda Fox. (Courtesy of Theresa Fox)

always be taken care of. In contrast, Gardner was not the kind of person who would try to push anyone into doing something they didn't want to do.

The same people in the comic industry that Fox developed a relationship with would also bond with his children.

According to a letter by his daughter Lynda Fox-Cohen, sent to comics writer Paul Kupperberg, Sheldon Mayer used to come over and help put together the trains for her brother on Christmas Eve.[23] Part of this is because Gardner Fox wasn't a handy person. In that same letter, she tells a funny little story about how his wife once asked him to hang a Winslow Homer print. Even though he did hang it, he hung it upside down. When his wife called him on it, the younger Lynda describes him as devilishly telling her that her mom wouldn't ask him to do those things anymore after that.

This moment gives a sense of the mischievousness Fox shared with his daughter. Asking Mayer to come over and help him certainly kept him from having to do more of that kind of manual work, but it was also a nice way of including him in their holiday celebrations and this closeness gives credence to Mayer's explanation of why Fox chose comics over the law.

Vincent Sullivan was a part of their family celebrations as well. In fact, Gardner made him Jeffrey's godfather. The main reason given for this is that Sullivan's wife had a miscarriage earlier in the year, making this an especially kind thing to do for his friend and fellow Catholic.

Once Gardner decided to specialize in writing comics for his livelihood, he built a detailed and rigid schedule, which gave him the ability to maintain his impressive output. As such, he was able to be the man behind stories featuring a large number of Golden Age characters including Zatara, Hawkman, Flash, Skyman, and Doctor Fate. He even produced one Superman story. Many super-heroes of the time were pulp-influenced white men with various motifs such as the hero being a magician or a detective. Fox composed a fair amount of these as well as adding his special touch to the still-developing super-hero genre.

One cannot simply read an author's work and assume it is reflective of who wrote it; however, with his extensive output, it should be no surprise that he looked for inspiration everywhere he could, including his own life. This is clearest in the similarities we see between Fox and Steve Malone, but it can also be seen in many other characters Fox had a hand in creating at DC and other companies.

It was not just Fox's career that grew during this era of his life. He deepened relationships, made new friends, and somehow found the time to start a family. This would make him one of a few people in the comic industry in the same position as the concerned parents who would become a much bigger problem soon.

Still, Fox's star was already brightly shining, and his first taste of real success was sitting just over the horizon.

PART THREE

I believe in the brotherhood of man and peace on Earth. If I could do it with a wave of my hand I'd stop all this war and this silly nonsense of killing people. So I used the super-heroes' powers to accomplish what I couldn't do as a person. The super-heroes were my wish-fulfillment figures for benefiting the world.

—Gardner Fox[1]

CHAPTER SIX

An All-Star Humanitarian During War

After the bombing of Pearl Harbor, on December 7, 1941, America and its brave comic book heroes rushed to join World War II. Even though America was officially neutral before that point, many of the big-title comic book heroes were already discreetly fighting racially caricatured, yet unlabeled, Nazi soldiers, Japanese spies, and Italian fascists. This was, in part, informed by the large number of Jews in the early comic book industry, making these issues more than simply political for them. Additionally, there was still a dismissal of comics as a medium, thus allowing more freedom to include such sensitive subjects than might otherwise be possible.

The comics containing the very first super-hero team, known as the Justice Society of America (JSA), were no different. In fact, nine weeks before Pearl Harbor, the title carrying the JSA, *All-Star Comics* #9, went so far as to mention Hitler by name.

The JSA is widely considered to be the pinnacle of Gardner Fox's comic writing and it is most representative of his work as a whole. Through the JSA, he explored issues surrounding war such as racial and religious hatred, starving civilians, and even war-orphaned children. For Fox, addressing these subjects represented a quest for justice.

Gardner Fox's understanding of justice is based heavily on individual freedom and equal treatment. This is very much in line with the way World War II was promoted as a moral war

America should be fighting in for the greater good. That said, Fox believed all peoples could be "members of a world wide fraternity of fighters for freedom."[2] This contextualized the propaganda-like material touting these beliefs and, because these comics were so widely read, informed American's understanding of justice amid this highly patriotic time. During the Golden Age, comics were everywhere in the US and even in the back pockets of soldiers overseas.

More than anything, though, Fox's writing of the JSA was tied to his core beliefs. As a Catholic who believed in service to others, and because he was unable to serve in the military, he found writing to be a way of enacting his values. It was through his writing of the Justice Society of America that Gardner Fox found an alternative way to serve his nation and all of humanity: writing comics that encouraged readers to help the war effort in whatever way they could while also trying to make the world a better place by encouraging readers to focus on our commonalities instead of our differences.

While *All-Star Comics*' Justice Society of America is a landmark series all on its own, it also set the stage for future super-hero teams. It was designed as an anthology title for less popular characters who hadn't been able to reach solo-title status. By putting these characters together, they could reach new readers.

In addition to being the first super-hero team, it was the first inter-company crossover because, while All-American Publications and National Comics both carried the DC symbol, they were technically different companies and the JSA featured heroes from both.

The original lineup included Fox's co-creations Hawkman, Sandman, the Flash, and Doctor Fate in addition to the Spectre, Hourman, the Atom, and Green Lantern. This changed as early as *All-Star Comics* #6 when the Flash was replaced by Johnny Thunder. Starman, another character Gardner Fox may have co-created, with artist Jack Burnley, joined the team in *All-Star Comics* #8.

It wasn't just the team make-up that changed. By the time Starman made it to the JSA, his gravity rod had been turned into a cosmic rod drawing its powers from the cosmic forces of the universe, thus making Starman an early example of a rebooted character much like Doctor Fate and Sandman. This gave Fox practice in how to mange these types of character overhauls, which would become fairly standard practice in the Silver Age.

Gardner Fox's explorations of justice and equality took on more meaning through a team of very different people who worked together as friends. This idea of people of various backgrounds coming together to save the world reflected America at the time.

When America officially entered the war, Gardner wanted to continue the military legacy of his family; unfortunately, he was unable to join, which forced him to seek out other means to serve his country. It should be no surprise that he tried to enlist in the army given that he surrounded himself with various militaristic touchstones such as the soldiers on the wallpaper in his office and the military miniatures he painted. After much excitement, Gardner sadly received a 4F rejection labeling him unfit for military service because of his color blindness and otherwise 'horrible eyesight.'"

This was understandably a sore spot for him. Like many who received a 4F, he felt a combination of anger and embarrassment over not being able to serve his country. According to family lore, the day he went off the join the army was very dramatic, complete with a tearful goodbye from his wife. Everyone expected him to be a war hero just like the others in his family had been. It was quite disappointing when he returned home later that same day.

Thankfully, his grandson Greg Fox explains that in order to help assuage these feelings, he joined the Queens Division of the World War II Civil Defense.[3] After the bombing of Pearl Harbor, there was a rise in defensive strategies built around the idea of civil defense. These included everything from the building of bomb shelters and the setting up of protocols all the way to the simple distribution of emergency survival information and goods. Those who were unable to join the armed forces, like Fox, were often eager to join the civil defense. Fox felt proud to do what he could and kept his civil defense helmet in his attic with the other family heirlooms. Greg Fox used to play with it when he was younger and described it as being very much like the old helmets from WWI, after which the Flash's helmet was modeled, only it was painted white. This isn't the only connection between Fox's comic writing and the war effort.

Political issues were ingrained in the comic book industry, but most super-heroes did not actually enlist. The JSA broke that trend all at once in the very first issue after the bombing of Pearl Harbor, titled "The Justice Society Joins the War on Japan!" by having every living member join the military.

Because it was his vision that barred Gardner's entry into the armed services, his writing of Dr. Mid-Nite provides an opportunity to see how he was able to find another way to participate in the cause.

Dr. Mid-Nite's vision impairment was caused when a mobster threw a grenade into the room where he was working on a new anti-viral serum. He believed himself to be blind, but he discovered he was only blind in the light. In fact, he had developed perfect night vision. This is why he fights at night or with the blackout bombs he invented. He also invented special "infrared glasses" enabling him to see in the daylight despite the fact that he maintained his supposed blindness as a way of keeping his secret identity as Dr. Charles McNider.

In his solo story arc within the issue, a hospital on a tiny island outpost gets bombed and an army scientist named Dr. Benson is rendered incapable of finishing his work. Dr.

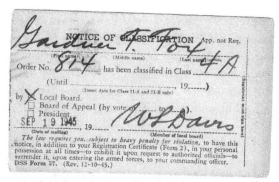

Notice of Gardner Fox's 4F classification. (Courtesy of Theresa Fox)

Benson insists that Dr. McNider is the only one who can finish the job. This allows Dr. Mid-Nite to join the Army Medical Corps, where he is able to serve his country by completing Dr. Benson's research by day and protect the island by fighting enemies during the night.

One can't help but read into this story a bit of wish fulfillment where some unique situation might have allowed Fox to physically serve. The thing is, he may not have gone overseas, but his work did.

Much like Dr. Mid-Nite, Gardner Fox did find a way to serve. Dr. McNider was able to complete the research of a fellow doctor and Fox provided a moral boost to the soldiers through the comic books he wrote.

Many people think of comics as specifically a children's medium; however, soldiers became a large part of the audience during World War II. Entertainment is essential to morale, and even though paperback novels were becoming cheaper and easier to find, the cost to make and ship them was still pretty high. On the other hand, a lot more comics can fit in a care package than books. They are also easy to carry, trade, and, because comics were thought of as throw-away reading, it wasn't as big of a deal if they got damaged or lost.

Comic books were essentially the perfect medium for a soldier's needs. In the introduction of *The 10¢ War: Comic Books, Propaganda, and World War II*, James J. Kimble and Trischa Goodnow discuss the war-time audience make-up for comic books, focusing on adult and child readers as well as soldiers. Referencing many other scholars, they present a string of data, such as comics outselling popular magazines 10 to 1 on military bases, comics making up an estimated 80% of overall army post reading material, and the army becoming the comic book industry's largest institutional customer during WWII. They even include a quote talking about GIs going to war with a rolled-up comic in their back pants pocket (17-18).[4]

Comic books provided soldiers overseas a sense of escapism while also allowing them a brief glimpse of what was going on back home. Comics produced near the start of America's involvement in WWI often emphasized community responsibility and pride in the military; they were filled with depictions of steadfast civilians taking part in the national war effort by scrimping and saving to support the soldiers overseas.

For example, along the bottom of the pages of many comics at the time, including the mostly war-free *All-Star Comics* #21, a stream of poetic line lines were included to inform readers of ways they can help the cause:

> Bottom lines on the following pages tell what to do while battle rages:
>
> Tin Cans in the Garbage Pile are Just a Way of Saying "Heil!"
>
> Waste Fats in Good Condition Help to Make Fine Ammunition
>
> Boys and Girls, Every Day, Can Give War Aid in Many a Way
>
> Every Time You Buy a Stamp, You Feed the Flame of Freedom's Lamp
>
> If You Have an Extra Quarter, Buy a Stamp to Make War Shorter
>
> However Far Soldiers Roam, They Want to Have Some Mail from Home
>
> Collect Old Paper, Turn it in—Help your Uncle Sam to Win
>
> You Can Walk into School and Store! Saving Gas Helps Win the War![5]

This list of rhyming lines are representative of the culture at this time. It shows the dichotomy between the patriotic pride of helping "Uncle Sam" by enacting these practices, as well as the condemnation and paranoia about those who weren't helping, as this inaction is directly equated to Nazism. Still, most of the lines remain proactive.

The Writers' War Board, who put together a Comics Committee to create characters and stories that would then be handed down to publishers, explicitly worked with creators to use comic books as a means of promoting racial tolerance within American society while also disseminating race-based propaganda, would have had a strong hand in the inclusion of these lines. They function as an exhortation-based instruction manual for children to follow in order to best support the morally approved war and the courageous soldiers fighting in it.

That said, it is through these appeals that comics also had the potential to increase morale beyond simple entertainment value by showing the soldiers all the ways civilians were working hard to get them home as safe and as fast as possible.

At the same time as soldiers were looking for civilian efforts and depictions of home, children were looking for any information about the war they could find.

Major events impact everybody and many parents will attempt to protect their children by avoiding references to things like a violent war. This leaves children to seek out books, comics, and other sources to satiate their thirst for important information. Despite this thirst, William M. Tuttle, in *Daddy's Gone to War: The Second World War in the Lives of America's Children,* explains that during World War II surprisingly few war titles for children were published and librarians' lists of books recommended for children included few books with war stories.[6]

So where did they inevitably turn? To comic books, of course. Comic books were one of the only places where children could read about topics that their parents may not have wanted to talk about, such as the holocaust, and it was during this time that comics were the most popular form of reading material for children and young adults in history.

Tuttle states, "Incredibly large numbers of children read comic books; of the homefront children between the ages of six and eleven, 95 percent of boys and 91 percent of girls 'read comic books regularly'" (158). In other words, almost every child was reading them, making what Gardner Fox wrote even more important. Although Fox was far from the only one being read, he was a busy man at the time because many of his fellow comic creators had gone to war. Sadly, Gardner's old roommate Bert Christman never came back. After co-creating the Golden Age Sandman with Fox, Christman served as a naval aviator in the Flying Tigers and died a war hero.

One result of all these children picking up comics was that their parents became even more worried about their possibly dangerous content. Because the concerned parents knew they could do little to stop their children from reading comics, their solution was to continue putting more pressure on the industry itself. DC had already developed its house code, to which their writers and artists were required to conform, and the "taboos" included many things commonly found on the battlefield: excessive blood, loss of limbs, dead soldiers, and sometimes even dead children.[7] Fox was one of the few people in the comic's industry who was in the same role as these concerned parents, because his son was one year old when Pearl Harbor occurred. Protecting children would have been very important to him, but, as imaginative as he was, Fox may have also used these restrictions as a source of creativity.

For example, it states that no child could be killed in the course of a story. If there is a war going on around them and no children are to be killed, what happens to them? This could have been the inspiration for *All-Star* #7, wherein the Justice Society of America raise $1,000,000 to help war orphans. At the end of the issue Fox even breaks the fourth wall by encouraging readers to help the refugee children in all the war-torn democracies in real life.

The house code applied to every part of the comic and during World War II the lines between advertisement, comic, and propaganda blurred. Advertisements and comics alike were filled with images of tanks, planes, and other battlefield equipment along with patriotic imagery such as eagles, the American flag, and the letter V symbolizing victory. Even if one did not pick up the comic and read it, the covers were essentially propaganda posters.

In *Champions of the Oppressed?: Super-hero Comics, Popular Culture, and Propaganda in America During World War II*, Christopher Murray explains the way in which propaganda can be understood as mythic because it works within a framework of values that are felt to be true within an exaggerated narrative. He states, "Consequently, super-hero comics, which were, using this definition, also mythic could easily act as vehicles for propaganda, presenting idealized conceptions of the super-hero who represents national identity in opposition to descriptions of the supervillan or enemy" (47).[8]

This theory explains why American comics were targeted for these kinds of messages. Indeed, at first glance, super-heroes like Captain America and Wonder Woman could be seen as propaganda-based in and of themselves, although in each case that reading can be subverted. Patriotism and nationalism were main focuses in many comic books produced at this time. Even if the main storyline wasn't based around the war, consistent inclusions kept it present such as short stories targeting a specific part of the war effort, puzzles highlighting past presidents, or even activities mimicking what a soldier might be doing, like deciphering a code. All of these were designed to encourage American pride in the children and convince them to help in the war effort just like their parents were supposed to be doing.

Fox balanced the nationalism the War Board emphasized by focusing on humanitarian stories. The features that would have helped in the war effort would have also been something he agreed with because of the kind of service-based person he was.

One of the key reasons Fox promoted these humanitarian messages was because of his faith. Fox was a devout Catholic. He never missed mass, prayed every day, and kept a prayer book on his nightstand until the day he died. Significantly, he even wrote using his confirmation name Francis for his middle name, thus showing his conviction to incorporate his religion into his daily life. It also allows us to apply this context to everything he wrote with that name.

One of the underlying themes in the JSA, in particular, is a focus on helping the less fortunate. This drive was encouraged in Fox's college years, where he attended a Vincentian school named St. Johns College. St. Vincent de Paul was a priest who believed a person finds God in providing service to others. As a Vincentian school, its main goal is to direct its "resources of faith and knowledge to combat the root causes of injustice and create paths to a more equitable world."[9]

This emphasis on equality mirrors the definition of justice Fox uses throughout his comics career. Through superheroes, Fox could imagine the way the world could be: a world where everybody tried to help everybody else around them. This drive to help is a big part of super-hero comics, as each hero must decide the best way to help depending on their particular skill set.

In addition to his service-based writing, Fox used his skills to participate in bridge and dance-related events though St. John's College to help fund Catholic priests in foreign missions.[10]

Ultimately, Fox was the perfect writer to tackle war-focused stories because his humanitarian drive was clear and his experience with including those messages made it possible for him to incorporate them into his storylines well enough that any propaganda-like aspects don't feel forced.

Through writing for the Justice Society of America, Fox was able to help by showcasing exemplars of justice and promoting the spread of humanitarianism.

In *All-Star Comics* #14, "Food for Starving Patriots!" he shows concern for hungry people in a world plagued by war. On the splash page, Fox sets up the story by explaining that Americans are known for their open-hearted generosity, but they are currently faced with a grave problem: they know any food they send to allies in occupied territories will be confiscated by Nazis, leaving many to starve. The solution is in the form of tiny capsules that can be converted into American-style meals such as steaks and a complete turkey dinner when sprayed with a secret solution. The JSA is supplied with these capsules and sent off to eight different European countries where they find ways to feed not just resistance fighters, but also children and captured allies all the while kicking Nazi butt. The inclusion of eight different countries gave Fox a chance to use his scrapbook for historically and culturally based references in each of the places they visit. Similarly, he includes current events he learned when he read the newspaper every day, such as a reference to Czechoslovakia being one of the first nations to "feel the crushing pressure of the Nazi war lords."[11] These educative tidbits are one of the things people growing up reading his comics fondly remember.

In a storyline with Hawkman, a "secret freedom newspaper" keeps patriots informed on the actions of Allied planes and reminds its readers that those planes only bomb military objectives. This plot point functions within the storyline while also working to minimize the panic felt by many living in war-torn countries.

Returning to Christopher Murray's theory on propaganda, this storyline is indeed presenting a particular set of values in an exaggerated narrative where the heroes are tied to national identity. That said, the storyline is just about as exaggerated as most of Fox's work. The values Fox is promoting don't feel heavy-handed or forced because these are the same idealized concepts of justice he puts at the forefront of a lot of his work. The JSA just happened to be a series in which he had the opportunity to explore them more explicitly. The fact that writers are seen as heroes serving their country also points to how Fox may have grown to see himself. Through this plot line, Fox makes the case that he is serving the country through the promotion of these propaganda-like messages of humanitarianism. This would have been an easy, logical jump for him, given his time working for school newspapers where he learned the power of the press. In this one issue, Fox's personal style is exemplified while drawing attention to important and often unseen issues surrounding World War II, as well as portraying the importance of words and the power they can hold.

Fox did not have to serve in the same mode his family did before him. He served his country doing what he loved. Still, these JSA stories have drawn some criticism in regard to race.

Gardner Fox's work on the Justice Society of America is a part of the Golden Age cannon, which includes problematic moments; nevertheless, the context is important to consider. Even later comics writer Roy Thomas, who is always quick to praise his friend, describes a reader in a foreword to a hardcover reprinting of wartime comics as "wincing" when they come across the Atom calling a helpful man a "good Jap" in *All-Star* #12 (3).[12]

According to Greg Fox, these racial slurs were commonplace in his grandfather's home. He states, "My father explained it as buddies breaking each others' balls and that there was generally no offense given or taken, but they would often refer to each other in derogatory terms [like] Jew, Mick, Guinea, whatever the other guy was."[3] They lived in a fairly mixed neighborhood in Yonkers surrounded by Irish, Italians, Jews, and other European nationalities, so there would have been plenty of opportunities for these slurs to pop up. Furthermore, many of the people Fox worked with were Jewish and his wife was the daughter of Italian immigrants. Fox grew up with many minorities and they considered each other friends. This resulted in a home where he would "in no way tolerate bigotry." So, while we see it as offensive to call a person these names, Fox may not have. This type of issue comes up again in a letter from Whitney Ellsworth and Murray Bonltinoff providing

Gardner with "helpful hints" like, "In some instances, oriental and gangster dialect is overdone."[13]

It could be assumed that at least some of this was a result of Fox's passion for research as he was trying to make the characters more authentic to his perception of what they would be like. Regardless, it points to a cultural awareness many white men at the time simply didn't possess.

Lamentably, the potential bias against those of Japanese descent is present in much of Fox's wartime work, with frequent enough use of terms like "yellow rat," etc. At the time, though, there was a lot of sanctioned demonizing and "othering" of cultures in the name of the war effort with the Writers' War Board behind a fair amount of it.

Gardner was forced to write what the Writers' War Board wanted, but he tried his best to at least soften their messages. They wanted depictions of America's enemies as incompetent at best and evil at worst.

One of the worst examples of this race-based propaganda found in Fox's canon is "This Is Our Enemy," which made no distinction between Nazis and other Germans while also asserting that World War II occurred because Germans were inherently violent. Undercutting this is the Flash's message, written in the gutter, that Germans have been taught to see war as a "purifying ennobling experience" and that they are "propaganda-fed" (47).[14] While the War Board was educating the masses about "evil" Germans, Fox argues that there was a parallel agency in Germany. Instead of supporting the war, he is suggesting that empathy and reason will naturally bring an end to it.

This moment was picked up on and mentioned by Rich Morrissey in *Batmania* #22. He remarked it was actually one of his favorite JSA stories, regardless of the obvious propaganda, because, "even during World War II you didn't treat the Germans as monsters the way so many comics did, but as people deceived and easily led by corrupt leaders." This prompted Fox to say, "Well, I always felt that way—that people everywhere are basically the same" (7).[15]

Repeatedly, this theme of equality and the benefit of working together appears in his work during this time. *All-Star Comics* #12, the second issue released after the bombing of Pearl Harbor, represents the kind of attitudes surrounding perceptions of Japanese people inside and outside of America. The cultural fascination and fear regarding Japanese spies covered everything from the Black Dragon Society in Japan itself to interment camps in the U.S. In this context, calling a person of Japanese descent "good" can be seen as a surprisingly radical act for the amiable Fox. While this is a minor form of protest, it still shows Fox finding a way to stand for the equal treatment of all people in a manner he was comfortable with, despite the fact that we now see it as problematic.

In addition to the formation of the Justice Society of America being one of the most important moments in comic book history, it is also seen as Gardner Fox's best work. Part of it could have come down to his perfection of the formula, which included a group introduction and conclusion as well as giving each member a short solo adventure in which to shine; part of it could be a result of the space he had to explore a story in the sixty-four pages given to him for each issue; part of it could be the familiarity he had with many of the characters due to the fact he had co-created half the team. I believe the biggest reason was that this was something Fox truly cared about. While there may or may not have been a touch of bigotry in his writing, his humanitarian messages shine through.

That said, comics at that time weren't just vehicles for a message. They also included information about how to help in the war effort. Comics helped sell war bonds, stamps, and everything else; thus, Fox was indirectly helping in a practical sense. As a result of all this helping of others, it seems as though he was able to help himself, too. After he received the 4F, it may have been difficult to work on stories with a setting that continually reminded him of what he was unable to do, but it appears he was able to find a sense of catharsis and purpose through it.

JSA stories remain important cultural and historical touchstones. Fox captured the essence of friendship and acceptance and those virtues are timeless. Fox claims he used the super-heroes as wish-fulfillment figures for benefiting the world. If even one person reading the JSA took the messages within those comics to heart, Gardner Fox did indeed make the world a better and more just place for us all.

CHAPTER SEVEN

The Wonder Woman Issue

Even if there are moments when Gardner Fox counteracts the understandings of gender roles at work in the time he was writing, his work is still a reflection of that time. The criticism most often applied to Fox's work is related to his treatment of women, with some going as far as to call him a sexist. This is mainly based on of an incorrect assumption that it was Fox's decision to make Wonder Woman the secretary of the Justice Society of America (JSA) and that it was thus his responsibiliy when she often got sidelined from the action. Wonder Woman is seen as the embodiment of feminism in the super-hero comic world and many people still count making her a secretary as the as one of the biggest crimes against her character and the most sexist moment in comic book history. While it is true he wrote the stories where she was a secretary, to judge or dismiss Fox as merely playing into female stereotypes limits our understanding of his writing as a whole.

There are many factors that led to the decision to make Wonder Woman the secretary of the JSA. In fact, the final decision would have been made by Sheldon Mayer, editor of both the Wonder Woman and JSA titles. It is also important to note that Dr. William Moulton, the creator of Wonder Woman, was very particular about his character and he did not want anybody writing her.

Marston created Wonder Woman in 1941, and Fox's attempts at writing for her show how the two men presented different perspectives on feminism. Moreover, criticizing Fox's writing of Wonder Woman based only on the fact that she was made the secretary of the JSA highlights the cultural bias inherent in the perspectives of this job and exemplifies a devaluing of women's work. While scholars are right to be attentive to the use of demeaning stereotypes that have long been used to keep women from access to power, the way in which Fox wrote Wonder Woman, as well as other female characters, conveys a sense of respect for women and their contributions to society in general; therefore, assertions that he was a sexist are not only misleading but inappropriately degrade the work of a man who was trying to accurately represent the women he saw around him.

Fox wrote many strong female characters who are just as capable as the men he paired them with, and his writing of Hawkgirl, originally known only as Sheira Sanders, provides a particularly important lens through which to view his writing of Wonder Woman.

One of the first things we learn about the Hawks is their life-transcending connection. Because of their reincarnation pattern, they have a level of respect and understanding of each other that goes beyond what would normally be possible. Similar to their patterns of rescue, Hawkman does often berate her near the end of the early comics, either directing these comments to her or thinking them to himself, but she makes many comments to him as well, such as in the Hawkman story in *Flash Comics #2*.

This story kicks off with Shiera figuring out what caused an earthquake, which results in a dinner invitation with the man who caused it; unbeknownst to Hawkman, Shiera packs his wings and a Grecian sword, prompting him to later ask, "What'd I ever do without you?" to which she responds, "You'd get yourself into a jam—and not be able to get out of it!" (24).[16]

This is indeed what commonly happens. In fact, the things that he often describes her as an "idiot" for doing are things that help him achieve his ends and mirror the kinds of choices he makes. There is undeniably a bit of sexism at play in the moments where Hawkman attempts to control his partner, or demean her, but given how often she returns these kinds of comments, they can also be seen as banter, in the style of the William Powell and Myrna Loy "Thin Man" films of the period. It can be seen again when he takes a souvenir home for his collection at the end of the issue and she retorts, "You would!"

Given what we know of the relationship Gardner Fox had with his wife, this is particularly enlightening. His grandson Greg Fox asserts that Lynda is responsible for the fact that the University of Oregon has the Gardner Fox Collection, as she "more than likely wanted [the materials] out of the house."[4] This drive to declutter ran in direct opposition to Gardner Fox's drive to collect. Because his wife would do the finished type work and revisions for him, this makes the retort work on two levels. Not only does it show a sense of familiarity between the two characters in the story, it could also be a self-deprecating joke shared with his wife. His mostly unique stance as a married man in the comic industry set him apart from many of the other comic book writers at the time. His life experiences gave him insight that they simply didn't have.

As helpful as comparison points are, in order to assess Fox's writing of Wonder Woman, it is also necessary to discuss the way that the creator of Wonder Woman, William Moulton Marston, wanted his character to be depicted.

While Fox was busy establishing himself as a go-to writer in the comic industry, Marston was calling that industry into question. Marston saw a problem with the way men and woman were portrayed in Golden Age comics and thought he could do better.

In *The Life and Times of the Amazon Princess Wonder Woman: The Complete History*, Les Daniels explains that before creating Wonder Woman, Marston worked as an expert on mental health for many different women's magazines. One of the topics he covered was the effects that comic books had on children. In particular, Marston pointed to what he saw as "blood-curdling masculinity" within the industry (55).[17]

His pointed critique of the industry caught the attention of M.C. Gaines. Fearing the growing anti-comics backlash, Gaines hired him to serve on an advisory board in a public relations capacity. Along with this offer, he suggested that Marston come up with a female character of his own. As a base, Marston drew from both of the women with whom he lived in a polyamorous relationship in his construction of this new character. Olive Byrne was a primary influence with her nurturing nature and the bangles that became Wonder Woman's bracelets of submission, but there are touches of Elizabeth Marston, with her independence and intelligence, as well.

In "Wonder Woman: Bondage and Liberation," Ben Saunders delves into Marston's psychological theories and makes the argument that, more than anything else, Wonder Woman is a reflection of those theories. In fact, there are indicators that Marston intended readers of his comics to treat them almost like instruction manuals.

Essentially, Saunders breaks down Marston's book *The Emotions of Normal People* (1928) into the idea that most men secretly want to be dominated by women, who are capable of enjoying both a dominant and submissive role with either men or other women. Moreover, because women are capable of taking up this dual positioning, experienced women should become "Love Leaders" and teach others, especially men, how to take pleasure in submission, thereby benefiting all humanity.[18]

The way in which Marston imagines domination and submission as both sexual and social forces also helps explain why bondage is such a common motif through his writing of Wonder Woman. Saunders claims that it is this supposed inherent female duality that allows Wonder Woman to be understood as a list of seeming contradictions: "For Wonder Woman is a fantasy figure who asserts, against the entire masculinist order, that it is possible to be both beautiful and strong, to be nurturing and independent, to be emotional and intelligent, to be assertive and kind" (70).

This duality is a key aspect of the character for Marston and one of the major factors that mark her as a feminist icon.

Gardner Fox got his first chance to write for Wonder Woman when she guest-starred in the Justice Society of America, and he showed himself to be fairly capable of representing the dualities that are so significant to her character. *All-Star Comics* #11, titled "The Justice Society Joins the War on Japan!" was not only the first issue prepared after the bombing of Pearl Harbor, it was also the first JSA story to contain Wonder Woman.

In her first solo adventure with the JSA, Diana Prince, Wonder Woman's alter ego, joins the ranks of army nurses along with Shiera Sanders. Fox even writes a whole page where the two heroic women chat. Even so, this page doesn't pass one of our modern tools to evaluate female representations in media, the Bechdel test, which came from the comic strip *Dykes to Watch Out For* by Alison Bechdel. In order to pass the test, a work must contain at least two women, these women must talk to each other, and their exchange must be about something other than a man.

It flunked the test because Hawkman is the topic of discussion during all the time that we can see them talking. Still, the fact that almost a full page is dedicated to showing two women talking is a pleasant surprise in Golden Age super-hero comics, which had very few female characters interacting with each other outside of Wonder Woman comics.

Showing his research on the character, Fox takes the time in this six-page solo adventure to include many important attributes that make Wonder Woman who she is. Right away, he mentions that she has the twin bracelets and golden lasso given to her by Aphrodite and includes her tagline, "The beauty of Aphrodite, the wisdom of Athena, the speed of Mercury, and the strength of Hercules," in both words and actions (22).[19] The explicit replication of the tagline in the story itself adds to the feeling that Fox is reveling in the extremes of her characterization. Wonder Woman once again makes a sympathetic and caring nurse, but she quickly discovers that the detachment she was sent to serve is outnumbered. As a result, she dons her costume and joins in the fight. She almost immediately turns the tables and gets the whole island under American control. This prompts the detachment she was helping to unanimously make her an honorary member. The mix of gentleness and strength shows that Fox was taking great care in representing the character.

Still, this version of Wonder Woman feels just a bit off from the Wonder Woman in Marston's comics. She is a touch more violent than normal, such as when she uses switches to keep the enemy soldiers in line as she marches them back to camp. Marston would have likely come up with some sort of rehabilitation through patterns of female dominance and taught male submission to prevent them from wanting to step out of line.

Similarly, her lasso is used more frequently and traditionally than in Marston's versions where he has her mostly capturing enemies to force them into obeying her and telling the truth.

Finally, she doesn't get tied up once. The motif of bondage-based instruction is common in Wonder Woman. This is most exemplified on Transformation Island, an Amazonian correctional facility where villains are taught obedience to loving authority, thereby giving them the opportunity to leave their villainous ways behind. This removes the submission aspects that were a key motif that Marston emphasized. These changes may make the solo mission more or less of a feminist text depending on how much one feels that those elements are a crucial factor.

Fox got a chance to write a second solo adventure for Wonder Woman in *All-Star Comics* #13, "Shanghaied into Space." Through his unpublished Wonder Woman script we can see what a Gardner Fox storyline based around teaching gender equality looks like.

The published issue, released after Wonder Woman's solo adventure was rewritten by Marston, starts out with all eight of the JSA members getting gassed by German agents during a meeting. Each member is placed into a spaceship and blasted off to a planet in our solar system, with Wonder Woman actually being sent to Venus. As he did for all of the other solo adventures, Fox starts by providing information on the planet each hero is sent to. For Venus, he writes: "Brighter than anything in the heavens but the sun and the moon, Venus reflects sun-light from the clouds that swathe her."[20]

Once on the planet, the setting is once again very much Fox with his pulp influences shining through. The planet is described like the jungle-covered Venus from the book *Carson of Venus* by one of Fox's favorite authors, Edgar Rice Burroughs. We can also see Fox's interest in history as men with spears are riding around in chariots, "not unlike the Assyrian war chariots" (65).

Wonder Woman soon discovers the Venusian females are "practically slaves" and an old woman tells her of a legend that one would come and free them. In order to help, Wonder Woman constructs a test to undermine the negative perceptions of women held by the men of Venus by matching them in feats of might. This plan is based on the men's excessive admiration of strength. While she is overpowering each man who comes along, there are several sports references, as is common in Fox's work, as well as an allusion to dancing when

Wonder Woman asks the king if she can "cut in." At one point, she even lifts the king above her head, causing him to exclaim, "You come from Earth! You would make me think women are treated as men's equals?" To which Wonder Woman replies, "Exactly!" After she bests all the attackers, the king is convinced that women are just as good as men and decides, "From now on, they take their places beside us!" (66).

At the end of the story, just like in all of the solo adventures where each hero brings home a scientific secret to help humanity, Wonder Woman is given "herbs," which are described as vegetables containing all of the vitamins known on earth. One could imagine Lynda Fox's love of cooking as inspiring Gardner to give Wonder Woman new vegetables to serve. Throughout the story, there are nods to Wonder Woman's prior comics such as a reference to "bullets and bracelets" and a mention of Hippolyte, Queen of the Amazons. This solo adventure shows her take on both traditionally masculine and feminine attributes, with equal value attached to each, ending with Fox explicitly stating that women are equal to men on Earth. Strictly speaking, it is a Fox-style female empowerment story featuring Wonder Woman.

This begs the question: what changes did Marston feel he needed to make?

William Marston rewrote the script because he felt Fox's original version did not accurately convey the purpose of Wonder Woman, who was a character designed to empower women through the means of his theories. Reading the Marston script Roy Thomas printed in "Two Touches of Venus" (in his comics-history magazine *Alter Ego*) instead of the finished product in *All-Star Comics* #13, we can see that, while many details are changed from Fox's version, Marston stuck with the overall outline in order to match the story with the other solo adventures.

One of the first changes he made is having Aphrodite direct the rocket to Venus. Aphrodite becomes a significant character in later stories, so this was a key inclusion in addition to his emphasizing of female agency. Once landed, Wonder Woman discovers that instead of the women being slaves to set free, the women are already in charge.

The main conflict comes from "terrible meteor men," who threaten the men of Venus. They aren't a problem for the women of Venus because the woman can use their wings to fly away. This is also how the women keep the men of Venus from treating them badly. The narrative rapidly brings in bondage and Wonder Woman seems to like being cuffed on the cheek by the man whom she describes as "so big and strong!" (68).

This moment is representative of many similar scenes of bondage in Marston's comics and runs in direct contrast to a moment in the unpublished script where Fox wrote Wonder Women as saying, "And don't play 'snap the whip' with me, because I don't like it!" Clearly, they had different ideas about what female empowerment looks like.

Still, there are more than a few mirrors to Fox's script. For example, when Wonder Woman stops spears with her bracelets, stating: "This is child's play compared to stopping bullets!" it is in reference to the same moment from the backup feature in *All-Star Comics* #8 that Fox mentioned.

In addition, Marston includes educative factoids about Venus, and a historical reference when Wonder Woman is celebrated in a traditionally Roman way. He also makes use of sports analogies and has Wonder Woman lifting a man above her head just as Fox did.

One of the biggest differences is the way the men refuse to fight fair in Marston's version. This makes Wonder Woman the upholder of proper behavior, since the meteor men are seen as cheaters whom she must teach a lesson. This difference is key. Thomas printed a letter Marston sent to Mayer along with the rewritten script where he states:

> You may remember at the very first, I pointed out that when you touch certain universal truths you create universal appeal. I ask you to note the universal truth in my script re. war and women taming men so they like peace and love better than fighting. This is the entire aim and purpose of Wonder Woman... (62).[20]

While Fox had a comparable message, the fact that Marston places the men in a morally lower position makes the "universal truth" Marston wanted to teach his readers more obvious. The story ends in a very Marston way with the women of Venus training the meteor men how to be more loving and peaceful, going so far as to have the men eating out of the hands of the women while they are chained to the floor. Wonder Woman finds this delightful, and Queen Desira kisses her earring so that she may guide Wonder Woman in making Earth men just as peaceful.

There is a strong sexual undertone in this exchange. Even though Fox's canon of written works does include lesbianism and explicit sexuality, this is one aspect of the character Fox avoided in his depictions of Wonder Woman. The omission in JSA is likely an audience consideration more than anything else.

Rather than nutritious and medical herbs/vegetables, the modified earring is Marston's scientific secret to help Earth.

Neither story is worse than the other. Each author wrote his script from his individual perspective.

In the end, Marston's solo adventure is the one that was printed without change in *All-Star Comics* #13. The issue ends with Hawkman expressing a desire for Wonder Woman to officially act as the JSA's secretary. She sees this as an honor even though it is a role she had already been filling, along with being a member of what has temporarily been rechristened the Justice *Battalion* of America. This results in a limiting of her inclusion in the title despite the fact she is still the first honorary member of the JSA who remains on active duty.

There were multiple factors leading to this decision and none of them had to do with Gardner Fox specifically.

The rewrite had to have caused more work than editor Sheldon Mayer would have wanted to deal with, and Mayer generally disliked having the level of control William Marston was given. As previously stated, Marston had a history of writing articles for magazines that were capable of influencing the public perception of comics, which is why M.C. Gaines brought him into the fold. Marston was subsequently known to amply praise Gaines. Exemplifying this, Marston even constructed a pen name for his comic writings out of a combination of his own and Gaines' middle names: Charles Moulton. These factors may have been part of what led to Gaines giving him a lot more liberty than other creators.

Marston set up Marston Art Studios where Wonder Woman's principal artist, Harry George Peter, and other creators produced his comics and Marston personally oversaw every aspect of the production. Having Gardner Fox write for Wonder Woman would have been an affront to his sense of control over the character. All things considered, it should be recognized that William Marston's limiting of Fox, and the rewriting of his work, which asserted the focus he wanted for the character, were protective moves more than anything else. Marston simply had a very strong vision of his character and wanted to keep it maintained across all versions of the character. Marston's need for complete control made working with him frustrating for Sheldon Mayer, who wasn't particularly happy to have Wonder Woman in the JSA at all.

When Robert Kanigher took over writing Wonder Woman after Marston's death, he reported in "Kanigher on Kanigher (and Everything Else!)" that "[Mayer] was grateful for my taking her off his hands. He hated her" (171).[21]

Another major factor was that the JSA had originally been designed as an anthology title to feature characters who didn't yet have solo titles. As a result, an in-house rule, referenced in *All-Star Comics* #5, explained that whenever a member received his or her own title, that character would leave the team and become an "honorary member."[22] This was put into practice when the Flash become popular enough to receive his own title, aptly named *All-Flash*.

Mayer would have been quite happy to invoke the rule due to the recent debut of *Wonder Woman* #1, in addition to her monthly appearances in the anthology title *Sensation Comics*, but instead, the publishers bent the rules when they decided to make her the secretary of the JSA. This allowed her to continue being a presence in both the introductions and conclusions, which was the right decision from a sales perspective. Wonder Woman had quickly became a popular character and would therefore help sell *All-Star Comics*.

In the end, the assertion that Fox was sexist because he made Wonder Woman the secretary of the Justice Society of America is easily refuted, as he had very little control over the decision nor was he in a position to protest it once it was made.

Even though Fox was unable to write many solo adventures for Wonder Woman, he did continue to write for her in the introductions and conclusions of many issues and this allows us to see how he dealt with writing her in the position of secretary for the Justice Society of America. Much like other creators used side-kicks, one of the ways in which Fox made use of the female partners in his super-hero comics was as an identification point for readers. The super-hero cannot be shown as scared or worried in the same way that a reader might be if they were in a similar position, but a civilian partner can. This allows an entry point into the work that may not otherwise be possible. It is shown quite often in his writing of Inza Cramer in Doctor Fate stories. Fox drew on his love of the pulp horror writer H.P. Lovecraft in his writing of Doctor Fate and Cramer's fears align with what Fox must have hoped the reader would have been feeling when reading those comics.

One example of this is in *More Fun Comics* #85 where Inza, as she does in almost every issue, insists Doctor Fate take her with him despite her fear and disgust, thus mirroring the emotions of a reader who is simultaneously drawn in and yet repulsed by the horror in these particular comics.

It is important to note that she is not looked down upon for her fears and shows herself to be helpful to Doctor Fate despite them, just like many of the other women Fox wrote.

This same positioning is at play when Fox writes Wonder Woman in her role as secretary for the JSA. Putting Wonder Woman in the introductions and the conclusions aligns the readers with her in that our responses to the member's solo adventures are echoed by hers both before and after they are taken on. This is most obvious in the conclusions, but the introduction to *All-Star Comics* #12 stands out for many critics.

One of the most famous panels used to argue for Fox's apparent sexism is on page four where Wonder Woman is shown to be watching the eight official members of the JSA rush off to ensure the delivery of key information to eight inventors. While the super-heroes set out, Wonder Woman watches with a "wistful look" in her eyes as she states, "Good luck, boys—and I wish I could be going with you!"[23] This moment of interiority is unexpected and conveys a sense of yearning that highlights her lack of ability to participate in their adventures because of her secretarial role. It also allows for the reader to empathize and identify with her emotions, much like they could with Inza Cramer, making this a particularly powerful panel. It could even be seen as a point of resistance in an industry that has not been consistently supportive of women.[24] The depiction of Wonder Woman's inner thoughts shows individual initiative. She is not just the stereotype of a secretary, she has thoughts and feelings just like any other character in the story.

This is supported by an often ignored prior panel on the same page. After Hawkman points out that there are eight inventors and eight members of the team, we see her taking the initiative by pointing out how she isn't a regular member and states that she will "remain at Washington to handle any emergencies that may arise!" The phrasing is important here as she doesn't ask if they want her to stay; she tells them where she will be and what she will be doing. She may wish she could be a full member who gets to go off on thrilling adventures, but she also knows her role at the home base is valuable, too.

There are many culturally based assumptions and biases that can come into play when one thinks of traditionally feminine roles and interests. This is particularly true when it comes to feminized work.

During the 1940s, being a secretary was considered women's work; initiative wasn't something men would associate with the job because these secretaries were told what to do, and they were supposed to be largely invisible while getting it done. This is what our stereotype of a secretary is based on and it can be very demeaning to those who do that work. An example even makes it into the film *Wonder Woman* (2017), where Wonder Woman equates secretarial work to slavery. In contrast, being a high-level secretary was considered a good job by many women at the time and they were proud of the skills and self-sufficiency they developed doing it.

Embodying this cultural perception, Wonder Woman sometimes does fit the stereotype, but there are also moments that run against it, such as those previously explored. In addition, the members of the JSA are shown to rely on her secretarial skills in several issues, and she is often praised for her work. It should also be noted that simply saying it is sexist to make Wonder Woman a secretary carries sexist undertones itself.

In "Working Girl: Diana Prince and the Crisis of Career Moves," Matthew J. Smith states, "And the crux of this line of analysis lies in the presumption that what a hero does for a living—besides being a hero—matters. And it must, for all of the choices our heroes make speak to their character and values" (152).[25]

As far as Wonder Woman goes, her values are based around her desire to help others, thus making nursing and secretarial work logical. In her secretarial role, she not only reminds her team- mates of important information, she also continues to be seen as caring and nurturing. Additionally, all of her careers have strong ties to governmental service which speaks to the patriotism that is a major aspect of her origin story.

Smith continues, "It is also about the reader finding access to the hero through their more modest connection to the rest of us" (160). In other words, it is the little recognizable moments in the fantasy that keep it accessible. This is essential because it encourages identification and self-reevaluation.

Another example is how a woman from the 1940s who loved to cook might feel validated when Wonder Woman brings home food because it implies that she may have been told how to prepare it and gives value to that process.

Our modern American society sees the expression of femininity as something that must be appropriately balanced and this is especially true when it comes to female super-heroes. In the same letter Willian Marston wrote to Sheldon Mayer in relation to the rewritten script, he addresses the overt expressions of femininity in relation to Wonder Woman's earrings. As previously mentioned, the issue he rewrote contains a moment where the Queen of Venus, Desira, kisses Wonder Woman's earring, giving it the power to transmit her voice to Wonder Woman, thus allowing the queen to direct efforts in making Earth men more peaceful. His final thoughts on the matter are that it "gives some point to the earrings, so any objectors to this style of female ornament will now excuse them on the ground that the earrings are wireless receivers" (62).[20]

This shows he felt that the inclusion of the types of ornament women often wear was potentially a contentious choice and highlights the difficulty in many of the choices these men made when trying to write for female characters in a culturally informed way.

In conclusion, many people may consider the biggest misstep in Gardner Fox's career as making Wonder Woman the secretary of the Justice Society of America; however, this is not something Fox was responsible for and any accusations of sexism as a result of it must be rejected. Through his writing of Wonder Woman, Fox showed he understood the duality which is a key aspect of Wonder Woman's character and promoted equality of the sexes much like he did with his other female characters. Not all of the women he wrote were fighters like Wonder Woman, but they were all intelligent women who were quite capable of taking care of themselves and others. Instead of trying to define a strong woman only through the inclusion of traditionally male attributes, like many writers do, Fox used the real-life women around him for inspiration, thus providing recognizable women for his fans to identify with.

Case in point, Gardner Fox's wife Lynda trained to be a secretary in her youth and did such work for him when he decided to become a professional writer. He was confident enough in her skills that his expectation was for her to be able to type up his finished novels in a couple of weeks at most. And this work was in addition to her other household duties. I'm not saying he never showed a touch of sexism in his work, but, whether the women were librarians, secretaries, or nurses, or whether they were scientists, detectives, or super-heroes, Fox conveyed a sense of value to the work they did regardless of its social status. In fact, it is the very moments that Fox is labeled as sexist that point to ways in which he is not. This attention to, and inclusion of, female characters is one of the positive impacts he made on the industry as a whole.

Under the moniker of Hawkgirl, Sheira Sanders has just as many, if not more, fans than her husband. Even Inza Cramer would one day become a super-hero herself when she took up her husband's mantel of Doctor Fate. These characters, along with others Fox had a hand in creating, have become paragons of feminine strength and continue to draw attention.

In the end, discussions of what makes a person sexist or feminist are simply not productive. We don't live in a black-and-white world and by limiting our view of Gardner Fox, we are missing the opportunity to see the nuances and positive steps he made within the complicated constellation of interests and forces throughout his substantial body of work. Much of the media products that came out during the Golden and Silver ages of comics was bigoted, but it would do us well to keep looking beyond the obvious to see what may be a moment of growth. Just one example of this is the way in which Wonder Woman's role as keeper of the history of the Justice League of America through scrapbooking and the like is enjoyed and shared by the whole team.

If all men in the comic book industry put in the kind of work Fox did in regard to his female characters, it would be a much more welcoming place for all readers, including the women who have long struggled to claim a space in this mostly male-dominated industry.

PART FOUR

I have found that during the bad times, the good guys are busier than ever because that's when the editors and publishers are very, very selective. Invariably, the people who are really good are inundated, because everyone wants top quality.

—Joe Kubert[1]

CHAPTER EIGHT

The Gilding Begins to Dull

Gardner Fox was riding high thanks to the World War II-fueled Golden Age, but the context for this success would soon end. Victory in Europe Day, often celebrated on May 8, marks when the Allies accepted Nazi Germany's unconditional surrender in 1945, thus showing a potential end to World War II and eliciting celebrations across the western world. One such celebration was located in New York's Times Square. While there is no proof Fox attended, he did go into the city on the seventh when the surrender was signed and marked "V-E Day" on his schedule again when it went into effect on the eighth.[2]

Regardless of where or how he commemorated this occasion, he most certainly did. After the Japanese surrendered on the second of September, the war officially concluded. This brought home drafted comic creators like Will Eisner, Harvey Kurtzman, and Jack Kirby, but the comics industry they returned to had taken a downturn. Over the next few years, comic book sales were decreased due to the increase in home televisions and other forms of entertainment. Instead of spending their hard-earned money on comics, children were able to spend their leisure time watching television programs their parents paid for. Further, a large part of the industry had been built around super-heroes, and the popularity of these super-hero comics began to wane because of their close ties to American patriotism. Leading up to the war's conclusion, war fatigue had hit in America and the soldiers who were in real-life war zones wanted escapism instead of a hyperbolic version of what they were currently going through.

In an attempt to keep readers, more fantastic stories slowly came to the forefront while the war became a background presence. The Justice Society faded further and further into the background until it eventually dropped out of existence. The damage had already been done, though, as most superhero titles had preceded *All-Star Comics* in being canceled. Without the war, many of these heroes lost their purpose.

Dealing a double blow to Gardner Fox, *Flash Comics*, carrying both Flash and Hawkman, was canceled with its last issue coming out in 1949. Comics were still a popular and successful medium, but the Golden Age had begun to lose some of its luster.

The decade encompassing the end of WWII and the formation of the Comics Code Authority at the end of 1954 was a fascinating time in the comics industry that sometimes get overlooked. Those still left in the industry persisted and companies were more willing to try new things in the hopes of winning back their readers. With the industry flooded with comic creators back from the war at the same time as titles were getting canceled, Fox was in a position where he had to branch out in various ways. Proving his versatility, he began writing in a wider range of genres, took on work from yet more companies, and even expanded the mediums he wrote in.

This medium expansion was enabled by the new relationships he formed during this decade. DC Editor Sheldon Mayer hired Julius Schwartz as his "story editor" in 1944 and Schwartz would go on to open new doors for Fox's pulp career much as August Lenniger would do when he became Fox's literary agent in 1950.

Although this decade may have been a tumultuous one for America and its comic industry, Gardner Fox proved himself capable of rising above the storm raging around him due to his adaptability and dedication to doing what he loved.

Fox's love of pulp magazines motivated his writing and the in-field experience Julius Schwartz brought when he joined DC enabled him to help Fox break into the same industry as some of his literary heroes. Having been an established literary agent for the now-declining pulp industry, Schwartz was a good fit for the comic industry despite his never having read a comic before being hired to edit them. There were a lot of similarities between the pulps and comics at the time, with some characters even moving between the two mediums.

This happened to be the same year Fox's Lovecraftian hero Doctor Fate made his final Golden Age appearance in *More Fun Comics* #98. As Fate would have it, when Fox shared his love of the pulp magazines that inspired this hero with Schwartz, he was rewarded with the opportunity to write for them, with Schwartz as his agent. In describing Fox, Schwartz stated, "[Fox] always thought like a lawyer—he was organized, meticulous, and he never walked into his editor's office without knowing what he was going to do."[3] Some of these same attributes could be applied to Schwartz, underscoring to why these two men were able to work so efficiently together.

From this point on, Schwartz functioned as both Fox's comic editor and also his pulp fiction agent.

Soon enough, Fox published his first piece in *Weird Tales* titled "Weirds of the Woodcarver." Coming out in September of 1944, the story has a complex structure and reads like a love letter to fellow *Weird Tales* contributor H.P. Lovecraft. One of its strongest aspects is the way it brings the reader into the story. It begins with a series of descriptions setting the scene, piece by piece, with many sentences starting with "there" and "here," allowing the reader to follow the narrator's gaze across the woodcarver's shop before he drops a "you," thus bringing the reader into the story and telling us how we are supposed to feel given what we have read.[4] This continues with the implied subject of "you" as we are instructed to look at a man, who can see secret thoughts, positioning the reader in a way that brings the story into the real world. It finally shifts to first-person perspective in the sixth paragraph where the story actually starts.

The story itself is filled with classic Lovecraftian tropes including Primal Ones existing before the time of humans and inhabiting a world barely separated from our own. When our journalist protagonist is transported to this world, the evil is so intense his human mind cannot fathom it. Doctor Fate would fit right in.

Interestingly, before he is transported, he recognizes what the woodcarver is describing and responds that he has read those books. In a very meta moment, the woodcarver replies that some humans have guessed the truth, thereby confirming Lovecraft's vision and gesturing to its supposed veracity.

Fox had dabbled in short stories before, but this new relationship opened up a fresh source of revenue in an industry he must have been very happy to join.

When it came to their comic work, Schwartz described Fox as being both a capable and reliable writer, and many consider the comics they did together as some of the best either of them produced.

The main way in which they did this was through "the Schwartz method." This method would start with Schwartz coming up with an intriguing cover idea that he would then give to Fox, who would use it to work up a possible story synopsis. From there, they would go over it and find a way to make it workable.

In *Man of Two Worlds: My Life in Science Fiction and Comics*, Schwartz states, "He plotted stories with me the exact same way, and he never sat down to write a story without knowing every twist and turn it would take."[3] They would get right to work figuring out all the major plot points and head out for lunch when they were done. Fox would consistently pick up the tab. Usually, they would complete the plots for shorter length stories in around three hours with book-length stories normally taking two sessions. Afterward, Fox would go home and write up the script. He always had it done by the deadline and came back with more ideas for the next story.

This method worked without a hitch, but one time a script came in from Fox with a major plotting error in it. Confused, Schwartz couldn't believe Fox would make such a mistake, so he asked him why he wrote it that way. Fox's simple answer was that the two of them had plotted it that way.

Guided by his time as an editor in college, Fox did not deviate from what his editors told him to do. From that point on, Schwartz would send him to the bullpen to type up the plot points they discussed before he left, so they could double-check things and avoid such mistakes from happening again. This did not shake his faith in Fox, though, and he considered the man an excellent plotter.

Still, when writers Robert Kanigher and John Broome, Schwartz' longtime friend, returned home from the war and needed work, Schwartz gave them the super-hero assignments they were familiar with and pushed Fox into other genres. Fox harbored no ill feelings. In fact, he quite enjoyed the science fiction work Schwartz gave him.

Shortly after the end of World War II, the Cold War began, and with it, new opportunities in the field of science fiction. The Cold War revolved around the mutual distrust between the United States and the Soviet Union. These global powers had been forced into a union because of World War II, but there were many political and economic differences. After the Truman Doctrine in 1947, which set a precedent for the United States to give aid to nations threatened by authoritarian forces, an arms race ensued with each nation trying to claim superiority through military might. This brought scientists, and science fiction, into the spotlight.

In order to capitalize on this, DC released *Strange Adventures* under the care of Julius Schwartz, a veteran in the field. The anthology series was heavily influenced by the era in which it was produced with most of the strange occurrences happening right here on earth. It achieved enough popularity that it spawned a sister series less than a year later, *Mystery in Space*, where the focus was more on interstellar stories. Fox wrote many of the stories in both magazines.

One of the most influential issues of *Strange Adventures* is 1951's "Evolution Plus! The Incredible Story of an Ape with a Human Brain." The story features a scientist who uses a cos-miray evolution machine to turn himself into a super-genius by moving up the evolutionary ladder. The story asserts that evolutionary development is curved and the scientist soon finds himself back at the start having to work his way up again. It isn't a particularly memorable story on its own, but there are a couple of things that make it interesting.

First, this is an example of Fox putting forth a scientific theory at odds with his strong Catholic faith. Second, this issue kicked off the trend of DC putting gorillas on their covers, thus placing Fox right in the middle of yet another celebrated moment in comic book history. The legend goes that the issue sold so well they decided to replicate the cover to see if it would sell again. After further success, it was decided gorillas were the reason and this prompted the placement of many gorillas on many covers. The strategy became so common Schwartz supposedly made a rule that only one gorilla cover per month was allowed.

Fox particularly enjoyed writing science fiction stories because he felt he could throw himself into them. Later, this would become literal when he wrote himself and editor Schwartz into *Strange Adventures* #140. As the Cold War continued, the genre would continue to rise in popularity, giving Schwartz and Fox the opportunity to work together for many years. In the meantime, westerns were filling the void left by the decreasing popularity of super-heroes.

Westerns were so popular in the 1940s and 1950s that the genre was taking over other titles in the comic industry. In 1948, *All-American Comics*, where heroes like Green Lantern and Doctor Mid-Nite were previously headlining, turned into *All-American Western* complete with a new cowboy hero named Johnny Thunder. Further, *All-Star Comics,* prior home of the Justice Society of America, changed into *All-Star Western* in 1951.

Gardner Fox wrote many a western; mentions of his new works in the genre would even appear in newspapers, and it was his new literary agent, August Lenniger, who facilitated these opportunities, starting with the prevalent pulp western magazines of the era.

Anytime a market becomes saturated, publishers can afford to get pickier about what they will accept. August Lenniger would report back to Fox with valuable information about what different publishers were looking for. Examples include *Ranch Romance,* the most successful of the western romance pulps, looking for more stories from a masculine point of view, while editor Micheal Tilden, at the pulp magazine *Popular Publications*, "absolutely require[d] girl viewpoint stories."[5]

Fox remained willing to write what was wanted, but there are still similarities across his work in the genre. His westerns are filled with men of unique ability learning a lesson like how to let go of anger. Their unique ability almost always stems from "Indian" knowledge or expertise. Fox uses the word "Indian" both as a derogatory slur and as a more benign descriptor of ethnicity. Similarly, the characters he describes as such range from exhibiting cruelty, like scalping, to more normal activities, such as kidding around with friends and gathering food. This range helps break down stereotypes as we see the way in which native people are often viewed in conjunction with his depictions of them being people just like anybody else. In other words, he undercuts the bigoted perspectives being put forth by providing more well-rounded characters and the tensions this causes are only made visible through the other's inclusion.

Likewise, Fox treats American history and folklore just the same as he does the history and folklore from anywhere else in the world. Fox also hits on all the classic cliches including casinos, ranchers, town brawls, and sexy women with secrets.

In order to support his family through his writing, Fox had to keep his productivity stable through a tight schedule, making whatever shortcuts he could come up with all but necessary. In addition to his scrapbook and other research materials, Fox also purchased a popular book containing mechanical story writing formulas titled *The Plot Genie: Western Story Formula*.[6] While Fox did use some of these formulas as a base for his work, the pages are annotated and he added many extra pieces of notebook paper with extra information akin to what comprised his scrapbook such as the lists of landmarks, slang terms, and historical data. He also taped clippings of various materials including panels of western comics on these pages.

Something that comes up with more frequency in the *Plot Genie* when compared to his other memory devices are his sketches. Fox didn't draw much, but he did make a map for his Kothar series and sketched out what he wanted Doctor Fate to look like, thereby making the mysterious character the closest Fox got to full creation. The most telling detail about Doctor Fate in relation to Fox's plotting formulas is the way in which his face is completely covered.

One of the many common themes appearing in Fox's narratives is the interrogation of secret identities. Fox often included people who knew both sides of his heroes, usually a romantic partner, and that information would strongly inform the way those people would interact with the title hero, thus transforming the narrative into an exploration of duality. Fox would also insert others, most often in a villainous role, attempting to

discover the secret identities of his title heroes. One can see why
this would be of particular interest to Fox who made frequent
use of pseudonyms.

Unlike the scrapbook, his personalized *Plot Genie* contains
many story ideas he randomly came up with titled "Plot Germs"
along with specific information that could be useful in moving
the plot forward, such as methods for signaling. The decoding of
a crucial message received from an ally persistently appears as

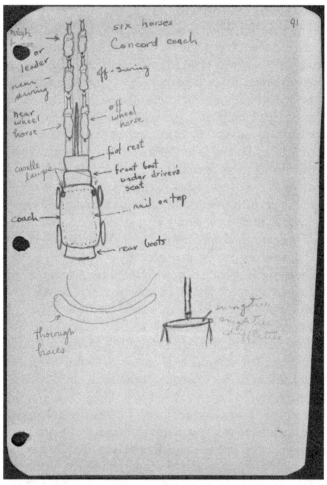

Gardner Fox's illustration of a six horse Concord coach
(Coll008_b0032_f001_001a, Special Collections & University
Archives, University of Oregon Libraries, Eugene, Oregon))

a pivotal part of his storylines. The use of information as a way of making the plot move forward makes sense coming from the always knowledge-hungry Fox. Much like time-pressed artists sometimes swipe images, the methodology this *Plot Genie* reveals is not as uncommon as one might think. Waiting for the right muse to show up is not always an option. That said, one never knows when inspiration might strike.

Sometime in 1951, Gardner Fox was laid up in bed with a bad cold and decided to start writing a novel in longhand because he felt he didn't have anything better to do. When he mentioned this side project to August Lenniger, he was given the go-ahead and kept at it. The book eventually sold via Gold Medal Books, making it the first of the 160 or so books Fox claims to have written.

Titled *The Borgia Blade,* it is a historical fiction story about a stable boy turned fencing master named Ilarion, whom Cesare Borgia brings into his cohort. More than anything, at its heart it is the story of a boy learning how to be a man and all the things associated with that. By the end of the book, Ilarion has learned how to think for himself, manage his temper, and treat women appropriately.

As to be expected, fencing takes center stage throughout this journey to manhood. Each bout is talked about in a way that showcases Fox's expertise; it includes the French terminology for specific thrusts and their counters as well as the exploration of realistic constraints and how they would require different strategies.

One of the most lovingly written passages is a description of the sword Leonardo da Vinci makes and gifts to Ilarion. The sword's scabbard is decorated with horse heads and enriched with both red velvet and tooled leather, but Fox knows the scabbard is not the most important part. Most of the praise given to the sword is applied to its blade, which glitters with an "azure sheen" and the "spaang" of its steel sounded like "an angel's voice."[7] All of this caused Ilarion to catch his breath at the sight while his fingers itched to touch it. Even his power of speech left him as he tried to stammer his thanks, only to squeeze the famous artist's forearm instead. Fox's passion for the sport is quite clear in these passages. Another passion made quite clear in this first novel is for putting the historical in historical fiction.

Fox took historical fiction seriously and would go to great lengths to make sure things were as accurate as possible. Historical fiction can be defined as a fabricated story with a plot set in the past complete with many details true to the period in which it is set. Novels in the genre often circle around a remarkable figure, allowing the writer and their readers to understand that figure and the surrounding events during the period they existed in through a new lens. The authentic rendering of these contexts is key, but Fox would take it a step further.

In an interview from the program book for Phil Seuling's New York Comic Art Convention, Fox tells a story about when he was writing a book titled *The Swordsman* just a few years after *Borgia Blade* came out. He decided he needed a map of Cairo from the year 1350. Considering public internet service was a long way off, this task proved difficult, but he did manage to find one in the Mt. Vernon Library. The librarians there weren't so happy when they would see the fastidious Fox come through their doors because, according to him, he was better at their job than they were. He claimed they would groan as soon as they saw him coming. He laughingly stated, "If I couldn't find something in their library, and I knew it pretty well, they didn't have much chance, either."[8]

This extended to vocabulary as well. Fox loved to use vocabulary as a way of conveying local color and this could prove difficult for his readers and himself. In this same luncheon interview, he recalled one problem word was "bursatrix." He was fairly certain he knew what it meant, but he wanted to double-check it before he put it in a book. Surprisingly, the Mt. Vernon Library had an extensive collection of dictionaries, including Anglo-Saxon ones. After Fox was unable to find the word, he finally decided to head over to the reference librarian. The poor librarians apparently spent around three weeks trying to find the definition and never did. Funnily enough, Fox provided the definition in the interview—a medieval term for a woman of the household who carries the spending money around in her purse—showing he did eventually find it on his own. These research skills were developed during his time at St. John's University, when he was studying to be a lawyer, and proved to be just as useful in his writing career.

One can see this attention to detail Gardner Fox put into his historical fiction novels starting all the way back to *The Borgia Blade*. The inclusion of Leonardo Da Vinci, for instance, is perfectly logical as Cesare Borgia did employ him as an engineer and military architect.

Operating on a deeper level, Fox's historically informed choices extend to the romantic aspects of the novel. Ilarion is very romantically minded and the form of romance he partakes in is largely Petrarchan in nature. Very early in the novel, Ilarion spots a cameo on the ground and falls in love with the woman depicted in it. This literally objectifies her in his young mind. His method of wooing stems from ballads that had been translated into Italian and they teach him to praise the individual aspects of the woman he desires while describing how he had loved her from a distance. When he actually meets the woman rendered in the cameo, she rejects these types of advances and he finds himself unable to treat her the way he had previously learned, thereby this form of wooing is called into question.

A final classical touchstone is the way that *The Borgia Blade* is loosely written as an epic, meaning it includes multiple elements of the form such as the fact that it starts in media res, contains long lists of things like the different types of ships, and the main character becomes a legend.

Many in the Fox family prided themselves on their education and Fox's novels gave them a lot to be proud of in comparison to his comic work. After the release of his first book, Gardner Fox's father Leon Fox sent him his "heartiest congratulations" through a letter dated May 1, 1953.[9] In it, he tells his son he stayed up until 11:30 finishing the book and that "it takes an exceptionally good book to keep me up that late." He continues: "You really did a wonderful job and your ability to portray action and wants so vividly should carry you far." He very much looked forward to this new chapter in his son's life and the future books Leon was sure were already "in the making."

Just a month later, Gardner Fox received another letter about the book from his mother Julia Fox, who wrote to the whole family. This is a much more detailed letter providing an overview of their day-to-day activities along with how they were doing. This seems to include a lot of gardening and playing cards. She explains that a store named "Jeffys" had to get more copies of *The Borgia Blade* because the store "sold them like hot cakes."[10] She then lists people who loved the book going as far as saying one person described it as "the best one he ever read." She also wanted to know when the next one would come out. They were very proud of their lawyer turned writer.

The fact that Fox had turned to writing historical fiction must have been a relief, as it was something they could all discuss without having to worry about the growing bias against comic books, especially given their traditional religious beliefs.

The nuns did not look kindly on comic books and believed them to be the devil's work. Fox's daughter experienced this tension first-hand. She was sent to a semi-cloistered school for disciplinary reasons and, because of the bias against comic books, he coached her to inform the dreaded nuns that he wrote historical novels when asked what he did. One day, the "meanest" nun asked her what her father was working on.[11] She quickly said he was writing something set in "olden England." The nun smiled, for once, and started listing off possibilities such as King Arthur or the Windsors. The poor girl felt forced into answering that her father was working on *Terror over London*. "Some guy, I think he was called Jack the Ripper." Of course, the nun stood horrified to hear this information. This bias against their father's work would turn some in the family against nuns even if they continued practicing Catholicism.

Writing these historical novels must have also been a relief for Fox because he finally had something he felt comfortable reporting back to his Catholic alma mater, St. John's College, for their alumni publications. The 1953 edition of *The Redman* states: "Latest news from Gardner Fox '32 reveals that he is hard at work writing historical novels. He has three to his credit at the time, as well as westerns and some science-fiction" (18).[12]

Fox always believed comics were a legitimate art form, but he also knew that the public perception of them at the time didn't agree. This held doubly true for those within the religion he held so dear. Thankfully, the pressure he felt never overwhelmed him because he had friends who supported his comic work.

While Fox was picking up work outside the comic industry, he also continued working within it, and his grammar school friend Vincent Sullivan expanded on the available options by opening his own company. Publishing new and original features was a driving force for Sullivan. This is something he tried to do at Columbia, but he was soon frustrated by the publications and policies of his partners.

In 1943, he finally seized his dream and started Magazine Enterprises (ME). He made original material the main focus and, proving the strong loyalty he fostered in others, brought on many of his friends. These were the same people who attended his bachelor dinner, including artists Fred Guardineer and Creig Flessel as well as the always dependable Gardner Fox. He also had Jerry Siegel and Joe Shuster of Superman fame working for him. Because ME didn't place its focus on super-heroes, the company wasn't as impacted by the downturn in their popularity. Regardless, the industry as a whole had begun to suffer, prompting the same kinds of experimentation occurring elsewhere.

Case in point: in 1953, *Redmask* artist Frank Bolle came up with an idea to use panel breaks and extreme perspective to give images a "3-D effect" instead of forcing readers to wear red-and-green-lensed "glasses" as the other companies jumping in on this trend did.

Some of the most important titles to come out of ME in the early 1950s were Fox's Sheena-like character Cave Girl, Soviet-fighting red-clad super-hero the Avenger, and the genre-meshing western horror character Ghost Rider. When Fox was brought on to write for Ghost Rider, he was not the flaming-skulled motorcyclist many are familiar with today. The original was a cowboy named Rex Fury. He dressed in white with black accents, complete with a full cape and a classic cowboy hat, and appeared to glow because his outfit was covered in phosphorus. *Ghost Rider* became a popular series, but this was short-lived due to the condemnation of crime and horror comics.

In relation to this growing opposition, one company would soon be thrust into the spotlight in a way that could have killed the industry as a whole: Entertaining Comics (EC). Fox did work for this company and its predecessor. Before they were ever "entertaining" they were "educational" and helmed by M.C. Gaines.

Maxwell Charles Gaines was a pioneer in the comic book industry. Mostly, Fox would interact with Gaines as an editor and as co-publisher of All-American Publications. This changed after Harry Donenfeld decided he wanted to absorb the company into National/DC. Donenfeld's partner Jack Liebowitz then bought out Gaines, who used the proceeds of the sale to fund the creation of Educational Comics. The only title he took with him to EC was *Picture Stories from the Bible*. This meant he had to come up with a lot of new material. Perhaps remembering Fox's productivity level and how many characters he had already created, Gaines brought him on and they (along with artist Sheldon Moldoff) came up with a new character named Moon Girl.

Moon Girl is very much like Wonder Woman, but with certain aspects, such as the importance of bondage, being scaled down. The first issue is set right before the start of World War II and the main character is an empowered and beautiful princess from an exotic matriarchal land with sensational superhuman strength, speed, and endurance. DC wasn't very happy with the existence of the character and it must have been especially frustrating for them because Gardner Fox had already written for Wonder Woman and Gaines was the character's previous publisher. These similarities did not diminish the stories the character featured in. Unfortunately, tragedy struck soon after her creation.

While vacationing with friends, Gaines, along with his friend Sam Irwin and his 8-year-old son William Irwin, decided to go on a speedboat ride on Lake Placid, New York. Another boat collided with them and Gaines reportedly threw the young boy into the back of the boat to save him. Sadly, he and his friend did not survive the accident. Gaines died on August 20, 1947. Fox described him as a great guy who "always had the interest of his writers and artists at heart."

When discussing what happened, Fox labeled it a "personal tragedy" (7).[13] Faithfully, Fox didn't give up on the character they created together and he continued to work for his son William when he took over the company.

When the younger Gaines inherited his father's Educational Comics, he changed the name to Entertaining Comics and released a "new trend" of comics including, among others, several horror, science fiction, and crime comics. The character of Moon Girl exemplifies these changes. In order to cash in on the popularity of crime comics, her title changed to *Moon Girl Fights Crime* by issue seven and the language changed quite a bit with words like "spine tingling," "vicious," and "blood thirsty" grounding the tales in their new branding.[14] This was unsuccessful and the title changed once again into the mostly unrelated, and Marie Severin colored, "A Moon...a Girl... Romance," in an attempt to appeal to romance comic readers." It was this title that eventually became *Weird Fantasy* in 1950, one of EC's science-fiction titles.

Along with writing more Moon Girl stories, Gardner Fox also tried his hand at some of these new titles. Fox had stories in the aforementioned *Weird Fantasy* and other titles including *The Vault of Horror* and *GunFighter*. Out of this work, *Haunt of Fear* #15's "The Mad Magician" is of particular interest. Inked by Wally Wood, the story's main antagonist is one of Fox's favorites: an evil magic-user. This magician is no Zatara, though. He falsely believes his magic is real and plans to literally saw a man in half, then put him back together in order to prove his imagined abilities.

Not only is the narrative somewhat familiar, it also provides another rare glimpse of a woman's interior thoughts. We can read inside a thought bubble that she is rightly upset about the traumatic experience she had just gone through; however, the imagery is of her bravely walking down the road in the dark, stormy night. Her internal struggles do not stop her from pushing herself forward in her attempts to reach the police and rescue her husband from the crazed murderer.

Too often, "strong" female characters aren't allowed to have feelings like sadness or fear. Fox's capability to make room for these types of emotions renders his characters' resiliency more meaningful. Interestingly, the horror in these comics isn't nearly as horrific as the battles he wrote of in his novels. This ended up a good thing because horror comics were quickly coming under fire.

Regardless of all the growing turmoil in the comic industry, Gardner Fox remained fairly comfortable getting work in other genres, expanding to magazine work and even writing his first novel. This allowed him to live a normal life, with he and his family moving into a new house on Crotty Avenue in 1953. When his family looks back, this is the place in Yonkers, New York, they saw as home. This was also the address most of his fan letters were sent to and where the occasional fan would show up.

From his visits there in the early 1970s, Fox's grandson Greg remembers it as an older neighborhood with a lot of tall trees. The house had a closed-in front porch, where a toy box was located, with the living room just inside. The living room was divided into two sides. One side had a TV and the grandchildren were allowed to use it freely. The other side was a more restricted area with the Ethan Allen furniture. The dining room was behind the television area with the kitchen off to the right.

Theresa Fox recalls that the kitchen appliances were fairly old, but remained in perfect working condition. I can't imagine Fox's wife Lynda putting up with a kitchen that was anything less. Lynda cared much more about material items than her husband, but if something didn't need to be replaced she would keep right on using it. She may have been society-conscious, but the two of them also lived through the Great Depression and were of a generation that respected the value of a dollar.

People today would say they lived below their means, but they were firm believers in self-reliance and would never risk running out of money for the sake of something new and extravagant. Thankfully, Fox's ability to write whatever was asked of him continued to be enough to maintain their lifestyle. It could be said this was a successful time for him despite all the growing struggles around him.

With all the major shifts in the lives of many Americans, the period surrounding the end of World War II can be seen as rather kaleidoscopic. The spread of suburbia began to take hold and this changed the ways in which Americans lived and saw themselves. This especially applied to women and children, whose joy at the return of the male figures in their lives was tempered when they were forced back into their previous roles despite the independence they had gained during the war. Frustrations were rising everywhere and the Cold War had only just begun.

Gardner Fox survived largely insulated from this, but he experienced a lot of changes during this period, too. He went from primarily writing super-heroes to finding work doing everything from western pulp magazines to funny animal comics such as the Three Mousketeers, J. Rufus Lion, and the Dodo and the Frog. Along the way, he started writing novels and even found the time in his busy schedule of writing and researching to move. This was also when he started to befriend his long-time editor Julius Schwartz and lost a friend in M.C. Gaines. This loss would have huge ramifications when Gaines' son took over EC and rebranded the company, which quickly became known for pushing the boundaries of what was considered decent in many ways, including the questioning of the status quo. This did little to help quell the ever-increasing concerns of those who saw comics as dangerous.

Fortunately, adversity can be the harbinger of creativity, and we are all lucky Fox and his contemporaries rose to the challenge, as there was a much bigger one ahead.

CHAPTER NINE

The Comics Code
Strikes a Blow

On April 21, 1954, William Gaines, son of M.C. Gaines and Entertaining Comics publisher, sat before the United States Senate. They showed him the Johnny Craig-illustrated cover of *Crime SuspenStories* #22 depicting a man with a bloody ax holding a woman's severed head by her still pretty blonde hair. Gaines was then put in a position where he had to defend the cover. He went so far as to describe it as being in good taste. His argument was based on the decapitation not being overly explicit because both the head and the body were placed so that the ax's damage is not visible and there is only a little bit of blood coming out of the dead woman's mouth. It went about as well as you might imagine.

This story from the Senate Subcommittee on Juvenile Delinquency constitutes the lowest point in what many consider the darkest day in comic book history. All things considered, the fault hardly lies with Gaines. It is likely the results of this Senate hearing would have been the same had he not been there. So how did it get to this point?

While concerns over comics were there almost from the start, the shifts occurring near the end of World War II exacerbated them. The rise in juvenile delinquency gave some just the fuel they needed. Lamentably, this became literal as massive comic book burnings took place.

In 1954, the comic book industry suffered its biggest threat when the ultimate comics villain, Dr. Fredric Wertham, released the misconstrued, yet culturally damning, book, *Seduction of the Innocent,* which condemned comics as the source of corruption in the once innocent youth of America. The resultant panic forced the industry to create a broad pre-emptive code that lasted for decades.

Fox stayed somewhat sheltered from the panic other creators may have felt because he did most of his work for DC, a conservative company that had never published strong crime or horror comics. He didn't have to deal with it at all when he was writing his short stories or novels. Still, he was surrounded by concerned people both inside and outside the comic industry.

It is through hardship and tribulation one learns what is most important, making these moments particularly illuminating. By analyzing the materials related to Fox's life during the time surrounding the establishment of the Comics Code Authority, we can attempt to understand Fox's thought process regarding the restrictions he dealt with; therefore, a deeper understanding of the man and his body of work is made possible.

Although comics sales were decreasing by the mid-1950s, especially for super-hero titles, they were still being widely read. According to Carol L. Tilley, in "Seducing the Innocent: Fredric Wertham and the Falsifications That Helped Condemn Comics," United States market surveys indicated that more than 90 percent of children and more than 80 percent of teenagers were reading comics during this time.[15]

There was a growing divide between the generations, and a rise in juvenile delinquency made many parents look for something to blame. With so many children voraciously reading comic books, a medium that many parents didn't understand, they quickly became the focal point. Everybody from librarians and educators to police officers and religious leaders spoke out in concern. American society seemed to be waiting for a lightning rod, and when Wertham's *Seduction of the Innocent* came out, on April 19, 1954, they got one.

Wertham was a German-born American psychiatrist who worked at the Lafargue Clinic in New York City, where he treated many troubled juveniles who became his clinical examples for why comics should be regulated. Not surprisingly, almost all of Wertham's young patients read comics and he imagined a link between these comics and the lack of his subjects' mental health and general well-being. While seemingly well-intended, it is now widely understood that Wertham's disturbing evidence was misconstrued and misleading. Nevertheless, his book sold more than 16,000 copies in the United States within six months. Wertham's apparent expertise in comics resulted in his being consulted for many hearings including the 1954 Senate Subcommittee on Juvenile Delinquency, which examined the supposed link between comic books and juvenile delinquency. This hearing temporarily changed the face of the comic book industry in profound ways, in particular the creation of the Comics Code Authority to ensure that the comics being produced were appropriate for the children reading them.

For the most part, creators like Gardner Fox had to either conform to this code or find outside work.

The defenders of comic books were essentially powerless to prevent what appeared to be an impending doom settling around the industry. One of Wertham's main sources for the comics he believed could negatively influence children were those produced by William Gaines' revamped Entertaining Comics (EC) with its new focus on challenging the status quo, whether through the depiction of gruesome murders or by putting a critical spotlight on racism.

Consequently, Gaines volunteered to testify in defense of the comics industry. Many have criticized his testimony; however, Christian Albrechts, a scholar of this historic event, argues the committee was simply a publicity event through which the general public could be convinced the government was taking the necessary steps to control a perceived threat to innocent children.[16] The fact that the event was widely televised supports this reading.

The hearing resulted in the joint establishment of the Comics Magazine Association of America on September 7, 1954. This association included members from the comic book industry's biggest publishers, with their main purpose being to reassure the public that comics would be a suitable product for America's youth.

In order to do this, while also preemptively curtailing governmental regulation, they formed the Comics Code Authority as a means of self-regulation. The code, essentially a set of restrictions modeled after the already existing Film Production Code, focused on promoting so-called traditional family values. Content that was now considered offensive included everything from poor grammar, to wanton women and excessive violence, to the inclusion of supernatural beings. They judged each comic and, if it complied with the code, it would receive their "Seal of Approval" on the cover. The comic book industry showed a huge drop in profits and many smaller publishers went out of business before this code was enacted. According to Albrechts, "The number of publishers declined from forty-two to twenty-seven" (264).

With a few exceptions, the surviving publishing companies soon discovered that retailers wouldn't sell their comics without that seal, thus resulting in more companies shutting down. Most noticeably, EC soon reduced its production to the now magazine length *Mad*, thereby avoiding the restrictions set by the Comics Code Authority.

This was a very stressful time for many people in the industry. Because so many companies feared they would be the next to go out of business, they stopped hiring and only kept those who had already proven successful at their current jobs. They were even forced to cut page rates for their creators in order to stay operational. Some of the most impressive creators at the time, including EC greats like Wally Wood, were being turned away. Fox was lucky in that, while he did lose potential work when EC dropped its comics production, most of his comic work was under the DC umbrella and he had established his versatility and productivity leading, thus keeping him safe.

Fans too were feeling stressed, as is evidenced by early fanzines, printed in the 1960s, which included interviews with comic creators who made reference to Wertham or the code. These fanzines also contained articles calling into question Wertham's assertions—some serious, some satirical. Even Fox's fan letters show this fear. One such example is from Robert Latona:

> The reason I write these fan letters (this is my 4th one) is that I, an otherwise normal person, am obsessed with the idea of becoming a comic book writer like you. The distressing point is, everyone thinks I'm some sort of NUT. I admit comics don't have the best reputation in all the fields of literature, but why

is everybody picking on them (perchance you read the book *Seduction of the Innocent*).[17]

As an established veteran at DC, Fox avoided much of the tension, but he was quite literally surrounded by it. Regrettably, I was unable to find a single comment revealing how he felt about any of the things that were going on in regard to this censorship. This led me to a search through his canon to see if I could find an applicable allusion.

Out of all his work, the Justice Society of America is most representative of Fox's ideals because it was where he could best explore his understanding of justice; therefore, comments within it can shed light on the kinds of beliefs he didn't otherwise feel comfortable sharing. One story that stands out in the context of censorship is titled "For America and Democracy." The plot circles around the ways in which internal saboteurs and spies are attempting to undermine the free speech Fox so clearly feels is integral to American democracy.

Fox's writing often requires heavy word balloons, but the ones in the introduction to this story are so sizable they almost overwhelm the whole panel. In one such example, all the reader can see is the FBI chief slamming his fist on the table so hard it moves the phone next to him, with the Flash (somewhat obscured behind the balloon) mimicking the motion.

It is stated that allowing such things as censoring newspapers paves the way for dictators to assume power. The team members are particularly happy to take on the necessary tasks to prevent this from happening. The emotion in this issue might reveal a bit of wish fulfillment. It also showcases Fox's educational purpose in his writing as he has characters doing things like encouraging people to fight against "isms" and showing how important it is to check sources before believing something.

The story ends with the heroes assuring the chief that they were only doing the work any American would do if given the same opportunity. They say this with the team facing the reader, giving it an exhortative context.

Even though the message must be taken out of its context (pre-World War II anxieties) in order to apply to the Comics Code, the message remains: excessive control of the media is a form of dictatorship, and that goes against what America stands for. In addition, media literacy and social awareness are necessary within a nation rooted in concepts of free speech and freedom of the press. Thinking along these lines, one would expect Fox to rebel against the code, but that isn't necessarily what his work shows.

Assuming his years writing for school newspapers gave him a strong belief in freedom of the press, as seen in his work on the Justice Society of America, it would be easy to believe that Fox would value expression over repression; however, other parts of his personality appear to have had a larger impact upon the way he handled this moment in comic book history. All evidence points to Fox fairly easily adapting to the new restrictions placed upon him.

Further countering the ideals he put forth in "For America and Democracy" is the comment he made in an interview with Rich Morrissey for *Batmania* #22, where he responded to a question about why he stopped writing for Justice Society of America with: "I never asked questions—I always wrote what they gave me to write" (8).[13] This cooperativeness could have stemmed from the fact that he had to learn how to write under some restrictions, thanks to the list of taboos Sheldon Mayer sent out years before the arrival of the Comics Code Authority.

These codes had many similarities—such as a ban on cursing, torture, or drugs—giving Fox a fair amount of experience beforehand. Still, given the seeming contradiction, I emailed the ever-helpful and knowledgeable Roy Thomas to see if he knew what Fox thought about this censorship. He responded that, while Fox might have commented on the Comics Code, he couldn't recall such a statement. Thomas went on to point out that it was likely Fox just accepted it, and that "[Fox] wasn't a firebrand or a boat-rocker."[18]

Much like telling his children to describe him only as a writer of historical fiction, Fox didn't want to cause conflict. There wouldn't be much point in speaking out against something he was powerless to change. Besides, he could write without those restrictions through other avenues. As far as comics go, he had to find a way to express what he wanted within the restraints being placed upon the industry. In other words, the soft-spoken Fox may have written whatever they told him to, but they couldn't tell him how to write it. This is most clear in regard to how he handled the restrictions placed on the supernatural, which is something that comes up repeatedly across his career.

The Comics Code largely disapproved of supernatural inclusions; therefore, tracing how Fox adapted his use to fit within the restrictions of the code allows a more personalized perspective of this moment in history.

Gardner Fox's use of the supernatural has been present from the start of his comic career. In an interview titled "Gardner Fox Adventures" in *Batmania* #22, Rick Morrisey remarks that Fox uses supernatural elements often and those elements are as similarly accurate and detailed as the scientific facts Fox also often included. Fox responded to this by describing his substantial collection of both fiction and non-fiction books featuring the supernatural. He seemed proud emphasizing that some of them were "rather rare" (7).[13]

Putting his research to use under DC, Fox wrote for Zatara, who was both a stage magician and a real magician who dealt with all manner of things beyond our natural understanding. Fox's writing of Batman was also supernaturally tinged, as can be seen in his two-part series that began in 1939, where Batman traveled to a Hungarian castle to fight vampires by using silver bullets.

Shortly after this story, DC cracked down on such inclusions; however, Fox was able to make use of his research materials for Magazine Enterprises (ME) where he wrote, among other things, *Ghost Rider*. When Fox took over, he amplified the supernatural aspects, thereby making it more of a horror comic. The new origin story begins with the character being visited by the ghosts of several famous western heroes such as Wild Bill Hickok and Calamity Jane. They teach him various skills and give him a white stallion named Spectre. Despite *Ghost Rider*'s popularity, the code's prohibitions fostered the cancellation of the character.

The way in which the adoption of the Comics Code impacted ME, with the cancellation of *Ghost Rider* followed by the release of the more child-friendly *Presto Kid*, is indicative of the impact it had on Fox's work as well as what happened across the industry as a whole.

While unconfirmed by the Grand Comics Database, the Ghost Rider story "The Beautiful Witch" shows enough similarities to Fox's other work, "Revenge of the Unliving" from *Vampire Tales* #1, for example, that I feel comfortable enough to include it as an example of his pre-Comic's Code output.

The issue tells the story of a girl who survives a group of Arapahoes raiding and burning down the ranch she lived on. They leave both her and her father for dead. Somehow, she survives; however, her mind had snapped. Her uncle takes her in, only to find she now finds solace in her demonic "friends."[19] As was often the case, the supernatural villains were just as illusionary as Ghost Rider's supernatural aesthetics. The uncle had been having his gang dress up as demons to distract from his continuing string of robberies.

The story was published the year before *Seduction of the Innocent*. Despite the fact that there were no real supernatural occurrences in the book, the depictions of the demons, the visible corpse of her slaughtered father, and the female witch being so beautiful it caused the men to doubt her evilness, would never have passed the Code. It also wouldn't have passed DC's code because of the skull on the cover, let alone the appearance of what is supposed to be Death complete with scythe. This more horror-infused version of the character was canceled in 1955.

According to Paul Green, in *Encyclopedia of Weird Westerns,* this is mainly because of the increased pressure coming from the Comics Code Authority.[20] There would have been too many changes required to keep the title running.

Shortly after, ME came out with *The Presto Kid,* which filled the newly opened slot in ME's lineup. Similar to Ghost Rider, the Presto Kid appears to have magical powers; however, instead of scientifically based aids, he uses stage magic. Appeasing the Comics Code, the Presto Kid also happens to be the only man in town who doesn't carry a gun.

Unfortunately, it was too late. Westerns were quickly losing popularity and ME subsequently canceled its whole western line up, including this new title. By 1957, like many before it,

Vincent Sullivan's Magazine Enterprises folded, thus ending more of Fox's potential future work. Luckily, comic book super-heroes had finally shown the faint beginnings of a resurgence the year before.

The public outcry against comic books had an eventual unforeseen consequence of refocusing the comics industry, with super-heroes once again leading the way. In the forward to *Alter Ego* #128, titled "Thanks For Nothing!" editor Roy Thomas explains that, without the Comics Code Authority cracking down in 1955, DC might not have felt the need to cast its nets as widely to make sales. Given DC's prior understanding that super-heroes should be exemplars for their child readers, it seemed like the perfect genre to revive under the pressures of the code.

The super-hero Schwartz suggested they bring back for the first trial run was Fox's famous speedster, the Flash. Wonder Woman, Batman, and Superman were the only super-heroes to survive the super-hero slump and Flash is arguably DC's fourth most popular; therefore, he was the optimal choice for revival. As it had been around six years since Flash had a running title, he would have been new to a fair amount of readers; however, instead of our beloved Jay Garrick, Robert Kanigher was tasked with coming up with a brand new Flash: Barry Allen.

Released in *Showcase*, a title where new features DC wasn't sure of could get a try-out, the Flash's new origin includes Allen getting hit with lighting and doused by chemicals. This gives him the ability to have the same super speed as his childhood hero. The sales on 1956's *Showcase* #4 far surpassed expectations; it was clear the newly enthusiastic readers were ready for the great return of super-heroes. Because of this, it could be argued the industry should be thankful for the fervor surrounding Fredric Wertham's *Seduction of the Innocent* because, without it, the industry may not have given the super-heroes we all know and love another chance; despite this, as Thomas put it, "Thanking Wertham is a bit like thanking the guy who pushed you off the dock so that you found out you could swim." (2).[21]

Delightedly, swim they did. The Golden Age may have ended, but the Silver Age had officially started. Regardless of personal opinions, neither of these events would have been as likely to occur without Wertham's influence, making him a very big part of comics history.

With these caped crusaders back in the spotlight, Gardner Fox found work in the genre again and the way he continued to use supernatural elements in these stories allows us to see how he adapted them to fit the restrictions of the Comics Code Authority. Their ban on the supernatural was mostly focused on creatures such as the walking dead, vampires, and were-wolves. That said, they reserved the right to reject anything they deemed contrary to the intent of the code; therefore, Fox always had to think about how his work might be interpreted. He demonstrated his ability to learn fast and found ways to work around their restrictions.

An example is 1961's "Secret of the Sinister Sorcerers!", the second story ever published of the new Justice League of America. Calling to mind the Presto Kid, the story's first setting is a stage magician's show. As the story unfolds, the reader is shown there are actually two dimensions, with ours operating through scientific rules while Magic-Land operates through magical rules. The magic itself is made safe through contextualization. Likewise, the main magic-user in this storylines is the fabled wizard Merlin instead of an alluring witch. Summoned by the super-heroes in the tale, they make light of the spell by talking about how ridiculous they feel doing it. The story prevents the reader from taking the magic too seriously at the end when an average citizen friend of the team named Snapper Carr offers to read his brother Jimmy a "real" story out of a book titled *Magic Tales*. The brother responds that he is too old to believe in magic (26).[22] This explicitly reminds readers that magic isn't real in this world.

These dismissive gestures must have appeased the Comics Code Authority enough to allow such things as Wonder Woman concocting a spooky witches' brew with ingredients like powdered batwings and the mummified foot of a frog.

These same techniques were used in Fox's work on a revived Hawkman, which still included supernaturally tinged Egyptian references despite the fact that the character's back-story had also been revamped. An example is 1964's "Attack of the Crocodile-Men!" When Hawkgirl is teleported out of the museum where the husband-and-wife team work as night guards, Hawkman follows the traces of radiation all the way to Egypt where it appears Egyptian gods are behind a string of thefts. Skirting any potential issues, the gods turn out to be mob agents in disguise. Ergo, these Egyptian contexts remain in a non-mysticized Egypt and there were no real supernatural threats like the mummies that might have populated a 1940s Hawkman story.

Once again, Fox was able to write about the well-researched supernatural contexts he loved while keeping them within the restrictions of the code.

Fox's career in comics runs parallel to many important historical moments and, while we can never truly know how he felt about the restrictions the Comics Code Authority forced upon his writing, we can see his resiliency during this time; as long as he had enough pages, he was creative and adaptable enough to produce whatever a publisher wanted. He developed these crucial skills through his many years of experience working for several different publishers who all wanted different things from him and were targeting different audiences. A pattern of taking what would be supernatural and making it safe through realistic contexts, thereby avoiding the vague restrictions regarding the spirit and intention of the code, is made visible. One could argue that it served as a creative challenge that prompted him to think about his established repertoire in new ways.

Even though a 'thank you' may not be in order, the restrictions following the release of Seduction of the Innocent made the comic book industry into what it is today, and Gardner Fox remains a guiding light in how to sustain one's personal freedom through such a trying time.

PART FIVE

I hope that you'll give the young readers of today some of your really thought-provoking stories—of the kind that were so important to the kids of my generation. 250,000 young people make up a pretty important audience. I suspect that you have at your fingertips one of the most important means of achieving the ideals of our society. I envy your role.

—Jerry Bails (in an early 1960s letter to Gardner Fox)[1]

CHAPTER TEN

Now Featuring Justice! On Earth 2!

After the disappearance of so many super-heroes in the 1940s, followed by the Comics Code Authority threatening to make the whole industry follow suit, it was quite a surprise that their return would eventually save the day. While still present, western and funny-animal comics faded from the spotlight, but science fiction became even more popular in the 1960s, with the genre working its way into others like the action/adventure comics that often featured super-hero stories. In part, this trend resulted from the technology boom that started in the 1950s where many items once considered luxuries became more broadly accessible. As a result, people experienced a mix of optimism and paranoia; the same technological advances that made it possible to bake a potato in minutes also produced bombs capable of destroying humanity as we know it in a fraction of that time.

The post-World War II arms race quickly turned into a space race as America and Russia each sought to prove to the other that they were in fact the superior nation. They went from competing with military firepower on Earth to claiming primary positioning for the exploration of everything beyond Earth. As people were looking to the stars for a glimpse of the Russian satellite Sputnik, their imaginations turned to what else might be out there. This is one reason that the flying saucer became an icon in the science fiction of the era.

In fact, thanks to the flying saucer craze, the comic industry found itself with its first profitable new super-hero since Black Canary in 1947. The success of Manhunter from Mars, whom we now know better as Martian Manhunter, is one of the sign-posts that marks the resurgence of comics.

Showcase #4 (1956) unofficially ushered in the new age with a newly developed version of the Golden Age Flash. The reintroduction of the Flash, with a new origin, identity, and costume, was exemplary of DC in this age when many characters were given second chances. In addition to writing new characters, this pattern would give Gardner Fox the chance to continue the work he had already started and update it for a new audience, thereby proving himself just as capable of leading the way in this re-creation process as he was integral to the creation process in the Golden Age. The beginning of the Silver Age provided Fox the opportunity to write some of his favorite characters, share his humanitarian messages, and shine that much brighter as a comic book creator.

Just a couple of years into the start of the Silver Age, and stemming from *Showcase* once again, Gardner Fox began to write for a new science fiction-based hero: Adam Strange. The character's memorable red-and-white costume was originally designed by Murphy Anderson, even though Mike Sekowsky served as the illustrator at the beginning of the series. Fox believed that Sekowsky wasn't as polished as Murphy Anderson, but he liked his work and thought that he effectively told a story with his art, something he found often lacking in what was then modern comics.[2]

Fox, together with Julius Schwartz, created Adam Strange in the same vein as pulp heroes like Edgar Rice Burroughs' John Carter of Mars. He was a human from Earth who gets teleported by zeta-beam to the far-away planet Rann where he adapts quickly, falls in love, and becomes the planet's champion. When broken down to its simplest points, it sounds almost exactly like the prior pulp hero; this prompted Fox to later explain: "I suppose you could probably say John Carter was in my subconscious" (28).[3]

Adam Strange was Fox's favorite character and he had tremendous fun writing him. Some of this fun came from Fox being able to let his imagination play when putting the character in all sorts of strange situations. An example is when Fox created the first living planet in comic book history, named

Yggardis, for Adam Strange to battle. I use the term battle loosely because we quickly learn that the sensitive planet is causing trouble out of a desire to have creatures live on it like other planets do. Strange discovers that the reason nothing can survive on the planet is because it gives off too much radiation. His solution is to separate the planetary mind from the planetary body to make a binary system that circles around a common center of gravity, thus allowing the opportunity for life to develop on half of it.

This story from 1960's *Mystery in Space* #60 illustrates just what kind of a hero Adam Strange is: yet another champion whose girlfriend fights by his side and figures out nonviolent, creative, scientific solutions that help his supposed foes instead of hurting them.

A big part of the fun Fox had writing Adam Strange was derived from the clever application of scientific theories and methods. Often, his adversaries were derivative of some kind of commonplace item that could only be defeated as a result of Strange's inventiveness and scientific knowledge.

In *The Comic Book Heroes: From the Silver Age to the Present,* Will Jacobs and Gerard Jones explain that this engagement provided an unspoken challenge to the reader, who would try to spot the "nemesis' scientific Achilles' heel before Adam Strange revealed it" (12).[4] Given the amount of knowledge this would require of the reader, it was not always an easy task; however, it was a fun challenge that mirrored how Schwartz and Fox worked together. This could have added a sort of meta layer to the enjoyment Fox had in writing this character.

More importantly, it exemplifies the educational focus that Fox consistently showed. Sharing his knowledge was important to him, and this gave him a chance to explicitly incorporate various types of scientific theories and methodologies in a way that children might remember.

Unfortunately, this kind of inclusion also created one of the biggest problems in regard to the sustainability of the character: villains could rarely make a reappearance once Adam Strange figured out how to defeat them.

A noteworthy exception are the two Dust Devils Strange defeated, first on Rann and later Earth. On Rann, he discovered they are high-temperature sodium-based beings, so Strange needed to add silicate, in the form of sand, to turn them into immovable glass. Then, a Dust Devil hopped a ride back to Earth with Strange and figured out how to make itself invulnerable to his previous methodology due to the differing conditions on our planet. Consequently, Strange had to come up with another way to freeze the monster: static electricity.

The lack of a rogues gallery may have hurt the character in the long run, but he remained fairly popular. Adam Strange would even go on to team up with another character of whom Fox was particularly fond—once that character was brought into the Silver Age, that is.

DC believed that its audience periodically reset due to age; however, the increased insertion of letter columns in their issues revealed a longer-standing fan base who, after seeing the revival of other popular Golden Age characters, started to write in asking for the return of others. Of these suggestions, the ones asking for Hawkman were especially impassioned. These letters revealed that, not only were the people who grew up reading comics still readers, but that there were refined, well-educated comic fans among them. In fact, several of them were teachers and students at both the high school and college level.

Clearly, Fox's educative style of writing found its audience.

All signs indicate Gardner Fox was happy to reintroduce Hawkman along with his heroic wife Hawkgirl. In order to give the fans what they wanted, Fox and Schwartz came up with a whole new origin, thus continuing DC's Silver Age pattern. The benefit of this was that they were able to largely avoid the previous Hawkman's Egyptian contexts, thereby side-stepping supernatural subject matter that the Comics Code Authority might frown on.

In this new version, the spellings of their names are changed to Shayera and Katar Hol, and they are turned into police officers from the planet Thanagar. They were sent to Earth to retrieve a fugitive criminal and then decided to stay on our world in order to learn human police methods. Originally illustrated by Joe Kubert, this series is still well-loved and, unlike with Flash, Fox preferred this Silver Age version. Some of this may have been how much he enjoyed writing science fiction, but the art played a part as well. When talking about Hawkman, in a letter to Jerry Bails, Fox stated, "The art work by Joe Kubert is absolutely tops, to my mind."[5]

One of the more intriguing aspects this version of the Hawks reveals is what Fox considered to be the wholesome family values the Comics Code Authority so desired. The suburban shift is quite clear when we see Hawkgirl doing activities like gardening and playing with her dog, Penny—although they never leave the science fiction too far behind..

In "Battle of the Bird-Man Bandits!" Fox has Hawkman affectionately embracing his wife, calling her pet names and asking her to dinner. She protests because she has housework to do first. We then see her put on her Hawkgirl costume to fly up and happily clean their orbiting spaceship using Thanagarian machinery that echoes some of the new technological luxuries an increasing number of people were using to clean their homes here on Earth's surface.

Just like other works in the Silver Age, the Hawks rely on their wits and figure out creative ways to battle without having to use their fists or any other weapon that might seriously injure their foes. Mostly, they found ways to stun them, knock them unconscious, or otherwise incapacitate them.

The response to the new Hawks was mixed. Younger fans weren't as supportive and prevented the character from becoming a total success. Still, the older fans kept writing in to rave about the work the creative team was doing. These Hawkman fans would go on to do big things in the comic book world.

Team-up books were a major trend in the Silver Age, making it rather fitting that some see the arrival of a revamped version of DC's first super-hero team, Justice Society of America (JSA), as the moment when super-heroes fully returned to fray. Now known as the Justice League of America (JLA), both Schwartz and Fox claim to have come up with the idea for the name change. Fox claimed that he changed the name because he thought that fans of the National Football League and Major League Baseball would be better able to identify with the name, whereas Schwartz provided several stories about the change. One claim he makes is that he thought "society" sounded too much like a club. It should be remembered that

Schwartz is known to exaggerate his role, but it could be a situation where they each had input on the name change.

Either way, the name wasn't the only thing to change. Instead of a title featuring lesser-known characters drawn by their original artists, the JLA had cohesively drawn storylines and contained the company's major headliners. The initial lineup included Martian Manhunter alongside the new versions of the Flash and Green Lantern, as well as Wonder Woman, Batman, Superman, and even Aquaman. Much like in the JSA, the lineup changed over the years as other characters were revived or revamped, such as the Atom, Green Arrow, and Hawkman.

An additional character appeared regularly enough to eventually become an official member was the intended teenage reader's entry point, Snapper Carr. This was executive editor Whitney Ellsworth's idea; he wanted the new team to appeal to the recently emerging hip youth culture that had already proven to be economically powerful. Ellsworth wanted Carr to be modeled off the finger-snapping television character Kookie from 77 Sunset Strip. Fox had to write his dialog in a beatnik dialect that is sometimes rather distracting. Nevertheless, Snapper Carr does have his fans, and he did get some of Fox's better characterization in the series. This illustrates one of the biggest weaknesses within the series and one of Fox's as a whole.

While the JLA is well remembered and remains an important part of DC, it was not perfect. As previously stated, the reliably fast Mike Sekowsky wasn't always the most polished artist, but this proved particularly true for him while working on JLA. He considered it his most demanding job. The lower page count caused Gardner Fox to struggle, too. This change required a faster pace that didn't match as well with Fox's wordier style. He also had to replace the solo adventures, where individual heroes were given the space to shine, with pairs of heroes working together with little time for their potential interactions to be explored. Complicating matters, Fox admitted that he didn't regularly keep up with many of the characters' then-current runs. Instead, he mostly worked off of lists detailing the character's friends, powers, etc.

According to Fox, he attempted to show variation in personalities through differing levels of seriousness as is seen in a comparison between Green Lantern and the Flash. The latter wasn't always well-received, with readers sometimes arguing that Fox used too much of a "light touch" with him.[2] This, once again, shows the formulaic manner in which he wrote. His formula extended to the plot, too, which is expected due to the use of his modified *Plot Genie* and other memory-prompting tools. In this case, the heroes would consistently fall into some kind of magical or scientific trap leading to what seems like an inescapable situation until one of the heroes comes up with the perfect plan and the villain is defeated.

This humanitarianism was given a new context in that the team had become more diverse in interesting ways. Even though Superman came from Krypton, he passed for human even when in costume. The inclusion of Martian Manhunter, who clearly did not come from our planet, caused perhaps the biggest shift in perspective. It put the scope of their adventures on a much grander scale because it served as a reminder that the whole world was often in peril. The means of saving the world often came from the creative use of a team member's unique abilities, turning each issue into a celebration of their differences.

One letter Fox received from a fan of the JLA even likens his writing for the team to "morality plays," and Fox himself is described as "an unjaded Shakespeare."[6]

Long before the inclusion of humanitarian themes became popular, Fox put them at the forefront to counter what he saw as a lack of brotherhood. To be expected, this results in some of the same themes appearing in both his JLA work and his JSA work. One such theme is the treatment of those with disabilities.

All-Star Comics #27 features a storyline involving a soldier who loses his arm. He has a brother who uses a wheelchair and the loss of his limb allows him to reassess the pity he felt for his brother, leading him to ask the JSA to help cheer up a group of children with various disabilities. It ends with a suggestion that we must accept people who have handicaps, including returning veterans. There is a slight misstep as the last page falls into the super-crip trope with its list of famous people who have "overcome handicaps" such as Milton, Demosthenes, and Beethoven. Looking at the people chosen for this list, I wouldn't be surprised if Fox had some input in its production.

While glasses and canes appear often, and are used by both heroes and villains in many different ways, it is safe to say that Fox would have included more. An example can be found in a script for the non-DC comic Texas Ranger where Jim Hatfield encountered a villain named Nightcrawler, a blind gunman.

Fox's editor for this series, Jim Hendryx, sent him a letter stating that:

> The blind man villain is particularly bad, since this would seem to give a man of Hatfield's capabilities tremendous advantage, and I'm afraid the readers' sympathies would go to the handicapped one. In any case, a blind man could scarcely be considered a worthy adversary for our peerless boy and his stainless-steel biceps."[7]

These comments point to the way in which it can be hard to determine what the original intentions were, and who contributed what, but it is pretty clear that Fox didn't see blindness as a weakness in this case.

In "The Case of the Disabled Justice League," in *Justice League of America* #36, we see five of the team members become disabled in some way, ranging from Hawkman developing asthma to the strange merging of Flash's two legs into one. Each team member finds a creative way to overcome their disadvantages while a group of disabled children watch from afar.

The narrative is similar to the one seen in All-Star #27, and the story ends with the same resolution and the same examples of people with handicaps who made their mark on history complete with similar imagery. The first item on this resolution is that those who have a handicap should be treated equally to those with able bodies.

Even though the stories aren't perfect, they show that Fox was making an attempt to at least include disability in his explorations of equal treatment.

Fox repeatedly emphasizes equal treatment and brotherhood in relation to race as well. In the 1940s, propaganda-fueled fear led to Asian nationalities and Germans being strongly "othered." Fox was able to undercut some of this and wrote stories like "A Cure for the World" for *All-Star Comics* #22, where we get the character of Conscience telling the JSA that the way to overcome prejudice is through education.

In the 1960s, a different kind of racial tension was rising. In response to police brutality and other factors, members of the black community took part in the bloody Detroit Race Riot of 1967. The following fall, "Man, Thy Name Is—Brother!" from *Justice League of America* #57 came out. This issue touches upon some trickier issues surrounding racism that are still being discussed today. We are given three examples of not only racist behavior, but also the reactions to that behavior. In addition to many comments about brotherhood and the need to respect each others' customs and beliefs, the legend states: "Because of man's inhumanity to man, men have learned to hate one another. For this hate is something that must be learned! It does not come with birth!"[8]

This message, and its opposite, is particularly clear in the part of the story featuring a teenager named Joel, who loses his job because a rack of clothes was ruined when he tried to stop a crime. Joel assumes that his firing was linked to his skin color, and Fox has the Flash essentially tell Joel that he should give the owner time to calm down and that the owner might give him back the job once he realizes Joel is innocent.

The story has some surprisingly progressive moments despite a few missteps. In conjunction with Joel's comments like "Colored boys never get a break!" and "Me help you—The Flash?! But I'm a colored—a black boy—", it appears Fox was trying to show the devaluing of self that can occur within institutionalized racism and the way in which being treated in hateful ways can cause justified frustration.

While this spoke quite well to then-current events, Fox didn't need such a visceral prompt to write these kinds of tales. Another example is *Justice League of America* #15's more fantastical "Challenge of the Untouchable Aliens!" from 1962.

This is a story where three giant stone aliens come to Earth in the wake of several countries testing their newest weapons of mass destruction on the same day. The team assumes the aliens to be foes. In the end, we learn that they were actually trying to save cities in both our world and theirs because the explosions had moved the Earth into what will soon be the same dimensional space at the same time. Green Lantern puts things right by simply moving the Earth and the final sentiment we are left with is the idea that the people we think are our enemies might not be and that what our world needs is "simple understanding among men, no matter what their race, color or creed!"[9]

In addition to Fox's continued argument that education is the key to building a sense of brotherhood, the potential destruction that prompted that coming together can also be read, in a broader context, as a cautionary tale about the ramifications of nuclear warfare.

Propaganda remained prevalent as a result of the ever-escalating Cold War, but most of the attention stayed focused on film, leaving comics more freedom than Fox previously had under the Writers' War Board during World War II. The main drives we can see functioning in Fox's Cold War-era stories were related to exploring defensive means of preventing escalation instead of finding ways to win. One can imagine this kind of conflict-resolution style at work in his relationship with his more assertive wife, too. With titles like "One Hour to Doomsday!" and "The Menace of the 'Atom' Bomb!" many JLA stories kept the Cold War as an ever-present backdrop even if the war wasn't mentioned directly, and this started from the very first issue.

The first appearance of the JLA featured a global threat and, accordingly, invoked the real-life fears nations were dealing with now that a war could feasibly end with the annihilation of us all. This prompted an educational push to ensure the creation of better rockets and bombs, which now symbolized global power, status, and even the potential for stability.

Ramzi Fawaz addresses this point in "The Family of Superman: The Super-hero Team and the Promise of Universal Citizenship" where he develops a case study of Justice League of America stories from 1960 to 1965 that show heroism in the light of an ethical commitment to universal citizenship, which is incorporated within American patriotism. Without naming him, Fawaz notes how Fox's repeated use of scientific knowledge and ingenuity to save the day functions like a bridge between the heroes and the wider world they are located in.

The team's first appearance had been in *The Brave and the Bold* #28 and Fawaz does a close analysis of this issue within the framework of the critique of Cold War nationalism found in these stories. This is made clear through the enemy they face: Starro, a gigantic starfish-shaped alien. We might consider Starro to be exemplary of Silver Age silliness, but Fawaz rightly points out that "the depiction of a colossal starfish as a menace to mankind might have seemed ridiculous were it not for the real threat of nuclear holocaust in this period, which many assumed would wipe out life on Earth and mutate plant and animal life into monstrously large forms" (42).[10] Comics were far from the only place that giant mutations could be seen during this era. This ties to the idea of universal citizenship because Starro comes from outside of America in more than one way: it is an alien and it is first spotted under the sea.

The way in which the evilness of a villain is derived from their abuse of scientific knowledge or talent is a regular motif in Silver Age stories. Exemplifying this, one of Starro's main goals is to absorb the combined knowledge of America's greatest scientists. Although, just as the fear of something bad happening is linked to science, so is the solution.

In a very Adam Strange-like manner, the way in which the heroes figure out how to defeat Starro comes from Snapper Carr being immune to Starro's mind control. They discover that this immunity resulted from his use of calcium oxide turf builder, otherwise known as lime. Aquaman knows that lime is also used by oystermen to deal with starfish and, sure enough, they are able to use it to defeat Starro. It seems that the JLA didn't need to absorb all the great scientists to save the day. All they had to do to save the inhabitants of the world was pay attention and work together.

This makes Snapper Carr's inclusion, in a time when children were asking their parents for home chemistry sets, particularly important. It reminds readers that, even as the stakes became global, the focus remained human.

As much as the Silver Age is known for earthly stakes, Fox found a way to take his stories even further with the introduction of the multiple Earths. Once again, the Flash became the character who would kick off a whole new set of possibilities in the DC Universe—this time, with a crossover event that featured the return of Jay Garrick, the 1940s Flash. One of the reasons Flash became the chosen hero was that Jay Garrick had already, sort of, made an appearance in the Silver Age. Barry Allen had been shown reading a Golden Age *Flash Comics* issue back in his debut, in *Showcase* #4. The heroism therein inspired Allen and became the reason he took on the mantle of Flash.

Another reason was the character's popularity. Fredrick A. Wright, in "I Can Pass Right Through Solid Matter!": How the Flash Upheld American Values While Breaking the Speed Limit," explains how the Flash's most popular era coincides with the Cold War because the Flash embodied both the hopes and fears of Americans of that time; the Flash represents the possibility that a positive outcome could result from having a secret identity and being the victim of a science experiment gone wrong. More than that: "In the age of intercontinental missiles, when only minutes existed between their launching and their landing, who could indeed save the world from nuclear annihilation but a hero such as Superman or Flash?" (59).[11]

The latter statement could be applied to many of the members of the JLA, but the first part, along with Flash's optimism, make him stand out. This can be seen in the story itself, which feels similar to an issue of *All-Star* thanks to the return of the JSA formula with a problem presenting itself, the team assembling, the team breaking apart for solo adventures that advertise the hero that stars in them, and an end that has the team back together in order to save the day.

In this case, when the magician Iris hired for her fundraising event doesn't show, Barry Allen thinks fast and Flash replaces the act. While spinning a rope faster than the human eye can register, he seemingly disappears. What actually happens is that the speed at which he vibrated was sufficient enough to break through time and space causing him to travel to an alternate Earth, providing us with the problem. There, Allen gets Garrick to return to the fight against crime so that the two of them can cover more ground in their solo adventures. They come together at the end to take down the arch-villains before Garrick watches Allen vibrate back to his own time.

This issue links the older heroes with their modern counterparts, thereby keeping DC's continuity intact—at that point, at least. However, probably the most remarkable part of this issue is that "Flash of Two Worlds," introduced the concept of multiple Earths into the comic book world.

According to Fox, Schwartz came up with the idea of having both Allen and Garrick in the same book, but Fox thought up the parallel worlds part after seeing the cover. Fox had been playing with the idea of multiple Earths going all the way back to his first short story, "Weirds of the Woodcarver," from 1944. "Flash of Two Worlds" can also be seen as a crossover event, and it set off a whole series of event-driven storylines that are still going on today. With all that, there is still another aspect of this issue to discuss: it contains an appearance of Gardner-Fox-the-character.

The character of Gardner Fox allows us the opportunity to look at Fox the person from an alternative perspective. In the DC universe, we learn, Fox's stories are actually a result of him being mentally attuned or psychically eavesdropping on the various sources of said stories. The idea may have originally come from 1950's "Menace of the Shrinking Bomb!" in *Strange Adventures* #113 where editor Julian Sloan, a stand in for Julius Schwartz, asked writer Greg Farmer, a stand in for Gardner Fox, to dream up a menace-to-Earth story and it came true.

In the case of 1961's "Flash of Two Worlds," the character of Gardner Fox unknowingly channeled events from what we would later learn is Earth-Two, where all the Golden Age heroes live.

Gardner-Fox-the-character's biggest appearance was in 1962's "The Strange Adventure That Really Happened!" in *Strange Adventures* #140. Fox, the main protagonist, once again wrote a story in which there's an alien invasion of Earth, and then it happens in real life. In this story, he had already figured out how to defeat the aliens, but he forgot, and the script he wrote is found to be mysteriously blank. The story provides a behind-the-scenes peek at story production, with Schwartz smoking his trademark cigar and showing just as much attention to promptness as Fox was known for. Readers also get a guest appearance of real-life artist Sid Greene strolling by to pick up the story to illustrate. And we don't just a sneak peak at DC's headquarters. The story transfers to his home office where we see him doing things related to working from home, like pacing around and talking the story out.

We even get a glance at the back of his wife, Lynda, who affectionately calls him Gar.

One critique I have is that Fox was far more partial to cigars than the pipe he is depicted smoking. Instead of the larger ones Schwartz regularly chewed on, Fox smoked Eric's, which were cigarette-sized cigars wrapped in natural leaf wrappers. His office carried the scent of these cigars, causing mixed feelings for family members. The smell brings back fond memories, but it is also a reminder of the role these cigars had in causing his later stroke.

That said, the biggest criticism family members have of this story is the speaking mynah bird that plays a prominent role in its resolution. Both Gardner's nephew John Fogarty and his daughter Lynda Fox Cohen have stated that there was no such bird.[12] In contrast to this repeated assertion, a bird story did eventually "come to light," and the younger Lynda shared it with Roy Thomas, who reprinted the email in *Alter Ego*.[13]

That anecdote starts with Gardner Fox telling his children they could each get a pet. His daughter picked a little kitten from a neighbor, but Jeffrey wanted a horse. It was simply not possible to make room for the necessary stable and riding space, so he didn't get his horse. At a later time, the father and son duo went on a camping trip with the Boy Scouts and found a dying bird. Jeffrey felt sympathy for the bird and wanted to take it home as his pet. Because he would be helping a wounded creature, Gardner was more than willing to let his son save the poor bird and help nurse it back to health. According to his daughter, the bird "loved Dad to pieces."

Alas, the elder Lynda was not as enamored. Then, one day, it mysteriously disappeared. Gardner's daughter held the notion that the disappearance may have been prompted by the destruction of something. Regardless of whether the bird spoke, it seems this well-loved bird formed the inspiration for the bird in *Strange Adventures,* which, in turn, served as an inspiration for Major Mynah, a character seen in yet another super-hero comic that was re-created with Gardner Fox's input during the Silver Age: *The Atom*.

According to the family, the story is, otherwise, a fairly accurate representation. The depiction of Fox's office was recognizable with his desk, complete with typewriter, as the center point and a large bookcase also taking up a starring role in the scene, making reference to how "crammed" the rest of the room was with reference books of all sorts along with filing cabinets filled with different notes and scenarios. The desk itself is a departure from the original, which had a piece of green felt with assorted pictures on top, covered by a thick piece of glass. The change makes sense because a standard wood desk would have been much easier to depict.

In relation to depictions, Mike W. Barr in his article "Spotlight on 'The Strange Adventure That Really Happened!'" explains that the original script shows that Fox wanted his likeness to be taken from the Atom's second "tryout" issue in *Showcase* #35 where its text pages displayed illustrations of creators done by Gil Kane, including Gardner Fox, Murphy Anderson, and Kane himself.[14] This is the same template used in Gardner-Fox-the-character's appearance in "The Strange Death of Batman—Chapter 2," from 1966's *Detective Comics* #347.

The story of *Strange Adventures* #140 ends with an interesting quote given Fox's desire to make the world a better place: after telling Gardner-Fox-the-character that he needs to get busy and write a new story, Julius-Schwartz-the-character states, "You'll have to be satisfied with having saved Earth in real life— as you saved it so often on paper!" The phrasing of this makes it seem as though saving the Earth on paper is equivalent in some way to saving the Earth in real life, and this line of thinking can be seen in other ways throughout Fox's canon with its continual inclusion of educative and humanitarian lessons.

While we should never blindly believe that an author's personal views are always being represented in his or her characters, Gardner Fox repeatedly did make the same kinds of comments as his characters did, and he has stated that he made writing choices based on his personal experience; therefore, his body of work can be interpreted as being linked to facets of himself.

In "Distributed identity: networking image fragments in graphic memoirs," Adrielle Anna Mitchell engages with a seeming preference or reliance on the written parts of a comic and shows how the illustrations can tell a story as well. She does this by breaking the comic into its smallest pieces, which she believes to be image fragments within the panel. By looking at the culmination of these fragments found in autobiographical comics, she posits that a larger sense of the author's self-representation can be found.

According to Mitchell, "atmosphere and setting are more than likely to carry at least some...or a great deal...of the burden of conveying identity in autobiographical works, and that they, like figure elements, can be meaningfully networked" (227-228).[15] This networking takes those individual aspects of a comic, such as Fox's common setting of a library, and puts them together with other common aspects in order to derive additional meaning from them.

Fox did not do his own illustrations, but he did write detailed panel descriptions of the settings and important details for the illustrators he worked with, thus making this analysis possible. Books are one of the most common objects seen in Fox's work, and this makes sense given Fox's love of reading and the intelligence he gives his characters. Doctor Fate, research scientist Hawkman, district attorney Steve Malone, and librarian Batgirl are just a few characters contained within this subset.

Fox himself practiced law before writing comics, and his sister was a librarian. As a result, many of the settings are those from his real life. Locations that are featured across the Fox canon are courtrooms, home studies, high society parties, and university campuses. Networking these aspects makes it clear just how important knowledge is to him, as well as pointing to his own life experiences. This is further elucidated in the instances he writes himself into the comics.

Looking at "The Strange Death of Batman—Chapter 2," for instance, the information the words give us is his theoretical quality-control process where the character of Gardner Fox plays through a different ending of his story through the posing of a "What if?"[16] This shows the thoroughness of his writing method, but the depiction of his office gives us an idea of what kind of writer he is. Once again, we see a large number of books in his home office, and this time we get to see his research cabinet along with a more correct version of his desk, with its green felt, in the center of the room with a typewriter on top. Interestingly, it isn't all that different from the Golden Age Hawkman's home office—sans the plethora of weapons, that is.

The parallels seen in what Fox wanted to emphasize in his depictions of self, and in a multitude of the characters he wrote, makes it clear how much of himself he put into his characters and adds credence to the purpose behind his continual inclusion of educative factoids. Knowledge was important to him, and he wanted to do his part to educate those around him.

All things considered, Jerry Bails' hopes that Fox would provide just as many thought-provoking stories in the Silver Age as he did the Golden Age were fulfilled. Justice League of America stories regularly included the same kind human-itarianism so prevalent in its prior incarnation because of Fox's drive to help our society live up to the ideals he explored through his writing. One of the reasons that this worked so well in the Silver Age was that JLA tales often showed the whole world as being under attack by entities outside of it, making these stories about coming together to save humanity on a planetary scale. This also enabled the imaginative Fox to seamlessly insert science fiction elements within his super-hero comics. An example is when Jay Garrick was brought out of retirement through the addition of Earth-One and Earth-Two.

In addition to his comics work, Fox kept writing novels. The late 1950s and early 1960s showcased a large number of historical fiction romances being published and republished as he became more popular. Some are more "hot-blooded" than others, but most of them follow in the footsteps of *The Borgia Blade* with a young man falling in love with a woman while proving himself in some way, thereby resulting in an increase in both fame and fortune. Fox also made himself more visible than ever to his fans, which would soon have a big impact.

DC in the Silver Age might be most remembered for its bright colors and general silliness; however, these comics spoke to the fears of the nation at the same time as they provided glimmers of hope. It was also a time where the company solidified itself through re-invention, bringing some of our favorite characters to life within what are more recognizable story patterns. Meanwhile, a rival company was making even bigger changes.

CHAPTER ELEVEN

Meanwhile, Marvel's Massive Emergence

The start of the Silver Age put DC in the spotlight in a big way, but another company was coming into its own. Technically, Marvel started in 1939 under the name Timely Publications, but didn't achieve the same foothold as companies under the DC umbrella did in the Golden Age. For most of the 1950s, they were known to the public as "Atlas" comics—actually the name of Martin Goodman's distribution company. By 1963, they had become the Marvel Comics we know and love. This rebranding began in 1961, when Stan Lee stepped into a new role. Stanley Lieber (his birthname) had been working for Marvel from almost its beginnings, when publisher Goodman hired him in late 1940, thanks to a family connection. Using the pen name Stan Lee, he was soon writing comics, and within the year he took over the role of editor in full.

After severe financial reverses in the late 1950s had left Timely little more than a rump comics company, distributed by the DC-owned Independent News, big changes began in 1961, spurred by DC's recent success in the once-again fashionable super-hero genre. Marvel's undertakings were hugely successful. As Gardner Fox put it, Marvel's success was like, "a jab in the back to the powers-that-be," thus prompting them to emulate their far smaller competitor.[17]

The rivalry between DC and Marvel has resulted in a bettering of each company, and the differences between them eventually became less severe than we might expect.

We have the success of DC's headlining team, the Justice League of America, to thank for the creation of one of

America's favorite families: the Fantastic Four. The legend goes that Martin Goodman saw how well *Justice League of America (JLA)* was doing and wanted to capitalize on it. He told Stan Lee to come up with a similar team of super-heroes. Lee confirmed this legend in an interview with Michael Eury published in *The Justice League Companion*.[18]

Even though it wasn't his idea, Lee was responsible for determining of whom the team would consist and their powers. He had been considering a change in career at the time. His wife, Joan, suggested that, with nothing to lose, he follow his passion and try writing the type of story he really wanted to write. Working with artist Jack Kirby, the result was 1961's *Fantastic Four* #1, perhaps partly influenced by Kirby's prior DC super-hero team *Challengers of the Unknown*.

There are also some similarities between the Fantastic Four and the JLA. We get the same kinds of science fiction elements and in both there are revamped characters from the Golden Age, with a completely different origin story and identity, named the Human Torch in the Marvel title. The slight variations include an even more stereotypically feminized role for the single woman on the team along with a monster instead of an alien.

The similarities between *JLA* and *The Avengers*, which came out two years later, are easier to see. The story structure and scope is congruous, as are a number of the characters. The Avengers contain shrinking characters named Wasp and Ant-Man to compare with the Atom, a mythological character in the form of Thor to compare with either Wonder Woman or Aquaman, and even an overpowered green character in the form of Hulk to compare with Martian Manhunter. Once again, through Captain America, a Golden Age character is soon included on the team as well.

Interestingly, Lee claims in the aforementioned interview that he never read any *JLA,* but then points out some differences between the team books coming out of Marvel and DC, including the fact that he often changed the lineup, put more of an emphasis on the team members' personal lives, and added in quarreling amongst members.

Regardless of Lee's assertion, it is clear that there are many similarities between them as the companies continued to influence each other. This pattern can be seen in more than just their characters.

One of the biggest changes Marvel made was putting all their heroes in the same universe within the same continuity line, and DC decided to replicate that as well. By this point, most of DC's major characters had excessively complicated, and often contradictory, backstories not only because of the revivals in the Silver Age, but also because of earlier changes in the Golden Age. Further, there were many creative teams working on each title, causing variations to arise.

Luckily for DC, they had already laid the groundwork for a kind of house-cleaning in "The Flash of Two Worlds," in *The Flash* #123, where we learn that DC's Golden Age heroes still existed on Earth Two and appeared in the pages of comic books as Silver Age in-world media. This was possible through scripter Gardner Fox, who became a character in his own story, being able to pierce the dimensional barrier between the two Earths in his dreams. Reader response to this revelation proved overwhelmingly positive, so these cross-over event stories continued

The Justice Society of America (JSA) was mentioned in *The Flash* #129, titled "Double Danger on Earth!" and a year later *The Flash* #137's "Vengeance of the Immortal Villain!" showed the JSA officially reforming for the first time in the Silver Age. In 1963, Gardner Fox was put at the helm of the first crisis just as he was for the steps leading up to it. In a two-part JLA story titled "Crisis on Earth-One!" and "Crisis on Earth-Two!" we finally get both teams fighting together to defeat villains from what we the readers see as the Golden Age (the 1940s) and the Silver Age (1956 on).

Already showing a touch of continuity, Merlin's crystal ball, originally from the second Justice League story titled "Secret of the Sinister Sorcerers," serves as a major plot device as it allows the heroes to communicate with each other cross-dimensionally.

The story features dimension-hopping villains who force the JLA to also swap dimensions in order to come to the other team's aid. It is a well-written, fun story, but the impact it had on DC thereafter is what makes it such a key moment in comic book history. From that point on, annual meetings between the two teams occurred with the word "crisis" appearing in the title. This, in turn, led to the inclusion of even more Earths in the multiverse. The creation of the multiverse also allowed more freedom in general as any new characters DC acquired or created could be written right into the universe through the addition of a new Earth.

The experiment was a success, and it did help solidify their fanbase, even if their sales numbers weren't as strong as they once were. In other words, as well as this worked, Marvel continued to draw in a larger number of new readers. One of the biggest reasons why is that Marvel's stories were humorous, emotionally complex, and relevant in ways that the majority of DC's were not.

Marvel stories stand out for their exploration of super-heroes as people and their inclusion of real-life issues that those heroes must contend with. Stan Lee started this trend by giving his new super-heroes recognizable flaws and placing them in the same timeline as our own. Previously, most super-heroes were archetypal and exemplary of human perfection. These stories can be wonderful, and they allow for an examination of what those archetypes mean and why, but readers were clearly ready for deeper concepts. Under the editorship of Lee, readers were suddenly introduced to complexities and characterizations that were much less common in comics before that point.

A good example is Spider-Man, who was co-created by artist Steve Ditko. Through this geeky teenage hero, we were given stories about maintaining a girlfriend, paying bills, and managing the mood swings that would be expected given the circumstances the character found himself in.

On a larger scale, the Fantastic Four demonstrates a family struggling with these sorts of issues. Bickering was part of their dynamic, which marked a departure from the friendship put at the forefront of JSA and JLA stories. Including conflict and resolution patterns also resonated with readers, as sometimes family members don't get along, and this enabled readers to place themselves within the story even as they did indeed get more fantastical. Not only that, the family was allowed to age and change as the stories went on.

Likewise, it was more than just the super-heroes that seemed more familiar. While DC did cover topics like civil rights, Marvel talked about them more regularly and in an explicit manner that tied those conversations to events that were going on at the time. Character interactions with current and past events served as a way of connecting plot points and storylines to reality, making it that much easier to see the message being conveyed. This relevancy was key to what made Marvel Marvel, and it still is today.

Because relevancy was seen as a major difference between the two companies, and Marvel's readership continued to rise, DC began to include relevant themes in an attempt to join in on this trend. Green Arrow served as the flagship of this experiment, with mixed results.

First, they stripped Oliver Queen, Green Arrow's "civilian" identity, of his family fortune, thereby bringing him down to more of a street-level hero like Spider-Man. Queen's loss of affluence allowed for stories that dealt with him encountering the plight of the working class in a way he never had before. Shortly after, this was taken a step further when he was paired up with another green hero: Green Lantern.

The most famous issue of this run is *Green Lantern* #76's "No Evil Shall Escape My Sight!" (1970). In it, we get one of the most famous speeches regarding racism in comics when a black citizen asks Green Lantern about his work history. He explains that he has read about the hero saving people with blue, orange, and purple skins, but rightly points out that Green Lantern had never tried saving black-skinned humans here on Earth. This pointed commentary, which reflected the racial tensions at the time, drew mainstream media attention and awards as well.

The problem was, not all fans were enthused about this increased relevancy, or the way in which it was included. Case in point, the cancellation of the book about a year later was due to a lack of sales.[19]

Creators, too, had mixed feelings about the way relevancy had become a trend. During a luncheon at the New York Comic Art Convention in July 1971, Gardner Fox was asked if relevancy in comics was a passing trend and he responded:

> I think you'll always have relevancy, there's no question about
> that. ... How long can you push it? It's like women's fash-
> ions—they change. Relevancy is always at issue in a comic,
> and should be. ... I don't care what you write about—drugs,
> or white slavery,[20] or anything under the sun—as long as
> you make the story interesting. I don't believe that a comic
> book is the place to preach. I think stands should be taken, no
> question, but I still maintain that the story value, the enter-
> tainment, is the big thing.[21]

Fox wrote many stories that could be considered relevant, making his comment seem counterintuitive. Indeed, taking on prejudice and encouraging equal treatment is something he is known for. With this in mind, his comment makes two things clear about his understanding of those topics.

First, they are not relevant because they are timeless values that would be applicable in any era. And second, the story itself was as important to him as the message it contextualized. In his mind, taking a stand is needed; nevertheless, relevant issues change and preaching is not entertaining. After all, nobody will take in the message if they don't pick up the book.

Marvel's emergence in the 1960s made a major impact on the industry as a whole and especially on DC, given its leading position at the time. Marvel brought with it characters who were complex, flawed individuals and more explicitly engaged with topics like the Cold War and racial inequality. This appealed to the rising counterculture and helped deepen the super-hero genre. The days of exploring cultural ideals and secret identities within a closed universe suddenly felt limited.

Successful or not, DC rose to the challenge and experi-mented with things Marvel was doing. It wasn't a one-sided process, either. Marvel as we know it stemmed from DC's success. In the end, both companies benefited from the com-petition and it is likely that neither would be as successful as they are today without it.

Oddly enough, the two companies were much more con-nected at the time than we might think. Marvel's comic books were distributed by Independent News, which was wholly owned by National Periodical Publications (DC), so DC actu-ally made money off of their sales. Furthermore, creators such as Jack Kirby, Mike Sekowsky, and eventually Gardner Fox happily worked for both companies.

This does not mean that DC didn't feel pressured when Marvel started its rise. Fox even received letters from his fans asking him to expand on his character work and increase his humor to match what they saw coming out of Marvel. This pressure came from higher-ups, too. The humor Fox put in some of his Atom stories, for instance, was not his decision. Foreshadowing the division between DC and Marvel, he much preferred his super-heroes to be more serious and less argumentative.

In relation to Stan Lee specifically, he had an additional critique. Fox described Stan Lee himself as a genius. He even commented that young creators were losing their own style trying to imitate him. Things take a turn when he added that it was his belief that Lee wrote continued stories because they were easier, going as far to as to state, "When he couldn't think of a way to get the Fantastic Four out of a jam right away, he'd just let it ride until next month!" in an interview titled "Gardner Fox Adventures" in *Batmania* #22.[2] There is some truth to this, but it also points to the way Fox prided himself on his plotting of a tight single-issue story.

These Marvel-related pressures, along with the stress caused by his increased awareness of the value system at work in the comic industry, was starting to wear on him. Still, there were several high points ahead for Fox and DC as well.

CHAPTER TWELVE

Fame!

DC's choice to start revitalizing its older characters in the late 1950s, in conjunction with its comics' inclusion of regular letter columns, yielded unexpected results. The fans who had been reading comics under the DC umbrella in the Golden Age were still around and they had power. They were able to come together and create a fandom organized around the comic book industry complete with publications, events, and awards. This might not have happened without the help of Julius Schwartz and Gardner Fox.

Schwartz gave the venerable Jerry Bails a crash course in fanzines, and Fox is responsible with connecting Bails with a young Roy Thomas. This duo would go on to many projects such as making sure comic creators got the credit they deserve for their works. Their sharing of this kind of information helped others to learn more about comic creators as well, and this served as the perfect catalyst for the beginning of comic fandom in its current form. They were encouraging the growth of this culture at the same time as comic book heroes were making it into the mainstream.

The 1966–1968 *Batman* television show's popularity not only introduced the character to a larger number of people, it also influenced the comic book industry. The Golden Age of comics may have seen higher readership, but the Silver Age brought comics into the mainstream with Gardner Fox right at the center of it.

The story of fandom starts when student teacher and comics aficionado Jerry Bails reached out to Fox in the hopes of acquiring back issues of *All-Star*. He saw these issues as formative to who he was as a person, even telling Fox in a letter from

1953 that "I can say most sincerely that these issues were of great moral value to me personally."[22] Considering the fact that collecting comics, as opposed to simply reading them and then tossing them away, was not common in the Golden Age, Bails knew that Fox was a last hope in his attempt to collect a full run of the JSA stories Fox had written. After several letters and some persuasive compliments about Fox's recognizably high educational level, Fox wrote back, "You win, you win!" and sold what Fox believed to be the only complete collection of *All-Star* issues #1–24 for the total of $75.[23]

A year after he sold his collection to Bails, yet another well-educated fan, a college senior by the name of Roy Thomas reached out to Fox in the hopes of replacing his accidentally destroyed copies of *All-Star*. Fox wrote back informing Thomas that he had already sold them and provided him Bails' address, thereby kicking off the start of a friendship that would bring fanzines to whole new levels. At the time, neither of them knew that this letter would also open up a set of new possibilities for Fox when Thomas wrote back thanking him for his kindness, stating, "I will not forget your assistance, and I just wish there was something I could do to repay you."[24]

Thomas did eventually find himself in a position where he could make good on this wish in many ways. Thomas and Bails also became friends based on this sequence of letters, when Bails was kind enough to send him dog-eared extra copies of All-Star #4–6 to Thomas as well as providing other avenues for him to read the issues he was missing.

At the same time as Bails was writing to Gardner Fox, he was also writing letters to editor Julius Schwartz. In these letters, Bails displayed a strong knowledge of DC's comic history, along with the ability to ask solid questions and offer clever suggestions, which earned him an invitation to the DC office to meet two of his real life heroes.

Jerry Bails' February 1961 trip to meet Gardner Fox and Julius Schwartz not only changed his life, it changed the landscape of comic fandom. When Bails was younger, he had gone on vacation with his family in New York City. He had tried to visit the office on 480 Lexington Avenue then. He walked in and saw the giant painting of Superman hanging on the wall of the foyer, but never made it past the front desk. This time, he was personally invited. The cherry on top was when Bails got treated to a lunch with these two men he so admired.

It was during this time that Julius Schwartz shared his experience with science fiction fanzines and encouraged Bails to make one of his own, instead of merely publishing a "JLA Newsletter" that Bails was already planning. Richard Lupoff, co-publisher of a science-fiction-and-comics fanzine called *Xero*, had already informed Fox about these small amateur magazines in a fan letter and Fox added his words of encouragement as well.[25] After this lunch, Bails wrote to Schwartz and Fox that he was indeed going to, in partial repayment, create a comics fanzine titled *Alter-Ego*. He described it as being devoted to

The cover of the first issue of Alter Ego. *(Courtesy Roy Thomas)*

their past and current creations, designing it to promote the "Great Revival" of costumed heroes.[26]

He then proceeded to write letters to every fan's address from the DC letters columns explaining his vision for the fanzine. He even requested Gardner Fox provide him with the addresses of fans who had written to praise Justice Society of America. With a list of potential subscribers and contributors, *Alter-Ego* was ready for release.

The first spirit-duplicator-printed issue of *Alter-Ego* came out at the end of March 1961, and Fox's part in its creation got a clever nod as the cover carries a Roy Thomas-drawn image of the Bestest League of America (a parody of the JLA) fighting a giant robot with the help of a written work titled "How to Catch a Giant Robot by Fox." The response proved overwhelmingly positive. Fox in particular felt excited about the fanzine, and he wrote Bails to tell him that he had "enjoyed every word and all its art. So much so, please find stamps enclosed for the next issue."[27]

Alter-Ego was successful enough that it caused an explosion of comic fanzines, with many people making one of their own and Bails himself creating companion fanzines. In support of Bails, Schwartz even promoted *Alter-Ego* in DC comics and a whole community was soon born.

This community was on full display when Fox's co-creation Hawkman was repeatedly revived through a fan-led campaign. When Hawkman was originally chosen to return in *The Brave & the Bold* #34, Schwartz sent out advance copies to a selected group of fans in order to print their responses in the letters column with the second appearance of the Hawks in the next issue. Two notables who ended up in the letter column, dubbed "Hawkman's Roost," were none other than Roy Thomas and Jerry Bails. As much as these fans loved the Winged Wonders, sales weren't high enough, thus ending the try-out after three issues. Fanzines and letters touting the cause began to pour in through the "Save Hawkman" campaign. If there was any doubt about the collective power of these fans, it was now removed. The fan fervor was a large part of why Hawkman received an unheard-of two additional trial runs. The third of these was in *Mystery in Space* where he was paired with Gardner Fox's other favorite character, Adam Strange.

Not all the fans were happy because the new location came with a change in artists. Murphy Anderson did solid work on the character, but Joe Kubert's fans, Mike Vosburg in particular, were more than disappointed. But the team-up was fun, and Fox enjoyed writing it.

Comic fandom would grow into something bigger when the Academy of Comic-Book Fans and Collectors was officially formed. This group of comic historians and fans brought people together to celebrate the comics and creators they saw as worthy of praise and attention. The academy's goals were actualized in the form of conventions and awards. Roy Thomas had come up with the idea of an award just a few months after the creation of *Alter-Ego*. He named it after comic-strip hero Alley Oop, as he figured a caveman must have been the first super-hero if we look at it from a chronological perspective. The winning of an Alley Award demonstrated significance because it codified reader response in a concrete way that had never been done before.

Fox was nominated for many Alley Awards, and knowing his preferences reveals a sense of enjoyment that links the works that earned him a win. In *The Comic Reader* #45, a renamed spin-off from *Alter-Ego*, Alley-nominated works were listed and Fox took the time to underline everything that he had worked on in his copy, which was later donated to the University of Oregon. The total was 18 nominations in 1966 alone.[28]

His first win was for Best Single Issue for the multi-verse-opening 'Flash of Two Worlds' from *The Flash* #123 in 1961. It contained one of his best-loved heroes, Jay Garrick, and the insertion of a science fiction device he frequently used in his prior prose work.

A year later, Fox won two Alley Awards. The story that nabbed the Alley Award for Best Book-Length Story was an Adam Strange tale titled "The Planet That Came to a Standstill" in *Mystery in Space* #75. It is a well-deserved award even if only for the sake of seeing Adam Strange use his brains to save the likes of the Flash, Green Lantern, Martian Manhunter, Batman, and Wonder Woman in this sequel to *Justice League of America* #3. It must have been especially delightful for Fox to have been able to write a story about his favorite hero saving the day when so many others could not.

The second award was for Best Script Writer. Fox felt proud enough to mention this to those in charge at *St. John's University Alumni News* along with the announcement that he had published his 41st novel and his first novel-length science fiction story, *Escape across the Cosmos*.[29] In 1963, he won the Alley award for Favorite Novel. This two-part "novel" was the beginning of the still-ongoing crisis events otherwise known as "Crisis on Earth-One and Earth-Two" in *Justice League of America* #21 and #22.

Finally, "Solomon Grundy Goes on a Rampage," from *Showcase* #55, earned him the Alley Award for Best Novel in 1965. While the Flash foe the Thinker was Fox's favorite villain, the monstrous Solomon Grundy was also one that Fox looked back on with "favor."

On a panel presided over by Jerry Bails during the sec-ond-ever comic convention, in 1965, Fox reported that his main focus was often on the villain of the story: "I know that when I sit down to do a story, usually, I feel kind of inspired by the villain. I mean, I try to project his personality into the story if I can"(15).[30]

This is particularly clear in this Best Novel winner because Solomon Grundy can be seen as the main character over the team-up heroes Doctor Fate, Hourman, and Earth-Two's Green Lantern. The story doesn't bring any other character into the main story until page four, and the first page provides a re-creation of the original introduction of Solomon Grundy from *All-Star* #33, thus reintroducing the character for new readers and making it clear that this was his story.

Clearly, the stories Fox enjoyed writing tended to be the stories others enjoyed most as well. This dual enjoyment was put on full display at the 1965 comic convention.

Sponsored by the Academy of Comic Book Fans and Collectors, the New York City event ran from July 31 to August 1 in 1965, and is widely considered to be the first "full-service" comic convention.[31] Held in the Hotel Broadway Central, it was the location that garnered the only complaints. Fan and new comics writer Dave Kaler had recently taken over as the executive secretary and made the decision to keep the cost of the event as low as possible because many of the fans they were hoping to attract were teenagers and college students who aren't known to have much spending money. The hotel was so run-down that the building shook with every passage of the subway causing cracks in the walls. Making things worse, there was also an infestation of cockroaches and a record-setting heat wave.

Thankfully, plenty of professionals, fans, and those in-between did attend including big names like Roy Thomas (now on staff at Marvel Comics), James Warren, Margaret Gemignani, soon-to-be pro artist Jim Steranko, future comics writer Marv Wolfman, and Flo Steinberg. Long-time comics professionals in attendance included Gardner Fox, Bill Finger, Otto Binder, Murphy Anderson, Mort Weisinger, and Gil Kane.

According to Fox's granddaughter, Theresa, such an event would have been outside of Gardner Fox's comfort zone. He was incredibly humbled by acknowledgement and recognition, but the idea of people waiting in line to get his autograph would have been a difficult concept for the modest Fox. He didn't even like to be at the parties his wife threw. Still, he did attend and seemed to have a good time.

This good time was extended after the event. He showed kindness to Roy Thomas when Thomas began his own professional comics-writing career in 1965 and moved to Manhattan. Gardner and Lynda graciously invited Thomas to enjoy a sumptuous home-cooked meal at their home in Yonkers, an hour's subway ride away. That invitation became one of the young Missourian's most pleasant memories of his early days in New York City—even though by then he had quit DC Comics to take a job under Stan Lee at Marvel.

In addition to the typical comic-convention features such as movie showings and purchasing opportunities, the comics and their creators were celebrated with a cake, a costume party, and an award ceremony. There were also proceedings like a symposium on comic fandom and that Golden Age panel dis-cussion where Fox was given the ability to speak directly to a room of fans.

Fox sat on the earliest example of a creators panel where he and Otto Binder found themselves on an enjoyable trip down memory lane. Moderated by Jerry Bails, the focus of the panel was Golden Age comics, and it was listed as the first item on

the program. It was supposed to include Fox, Binder, and Bill
Finger, but the latter was running late. As such, he did not
take part in the first part of the discussion. Adding a bit more
unpredictability, Bails spotted Mort Weisinger in the audience
part way through the panel and invited him to join in.

The discussion that occurred was elucidating and ground-
breaking, but there was more behind the scenes. Binder and Fox
had a lot in common with each other compared to most comic
creators at the time. Binder started writing comics a few years
after Fox, but they were the same age. They were also friends
with some of the same people, loved and wrote pulps, wrote for
multiple companies, were married with children, and expressed
strong sentiments against racism. This commonality was on
display at the con with the two of them cheerfully chatting
before the start of the panel about how they couldn't remember all the comics they had each written. Their camaraderie
was also apparent during the panel as they were seen nodding,
making comments, and asking questions of each other.[32]

Still, Fox's competitive side did come out. Near the start
of the panel, when it was just the three of them, Bails asked
when they each started and what level of editorial input they
experienced, to which Fox made sure to establish that he was
writing comics before Superman's arrival and that his editors
never took over the plotting for him.

One thing they agreed on was how beneficial the change of
pace was between writing comics and novels. Binder expanded
on Fox's comments by adding in some history on the beginnings of the industry. He talked about when there were only
a few writers in the field, which forced them to sometimes
write two or three stories a day. That kind of pace would be
exhausting for anybody. It would then make sense for them to
branch out from comics as a way of refreshing themselves and
maintaining their desire to write.

The panel cemented Gardner Fox and the other panelists
as Golden Age greats in the minds of those who attended.
Nonetheless, they were contributing equally to the so-called
Silver Age.

With the return of super-heroes in the comics, other
mediums rapidly followed suit and one of the more popular

examples was the live action television series *Batman,* premiering in 1966. Starring Adam West and Burt Ward, this was not the gothic Batman that Gardner Fox helped mold in the Golden Age. It wasn't the Batman of the earlier part of the Silver Age, either. This Batman can best be described as campy. The show was often frivolously exaggerated so as to amuse the audience, turning Batman into a far more humorous character than in his previous versions. It was filled with bright colors, upbeat music, and simple lessons for its younger viewers.

The more serious two-part series opener was titled "Hi Diddle Riddle/Smack in the Middle." While Gardner Fox was not credited, script-writer Lorenzo Semple adapted it from Fox's *Batman* #171, "The Remarkable Ruse of the Riddler," which is the first Silver Age appearance of the Riddler. Fox had previously been enjoying himself writing Adam Strange, but he was moved to Batman because Adam Strange wasn't selling anymore. Unfortunately, his enjoyment of the writing process was further curtailed when he was asked to write in the same campy style as the show because that is what DC thought the comics fans wanted as well. There were certainly fans who enjoyed it, but not all of them did, and that included Fox. In an interview for *Batmania* #22, Ken Gale singles out the Fox-penned "The Penguin Takes a Flyer—Into the Future!" from *Batman* #190 as one of the worst he'd ever read, and Fox didn't hesitate to agree.[2]

The television program showed a steep dip in popularity during its second season, prompting television producer William Dozier to come up with the idea of adding a new permanent costar to increase the ratings for the third season. Specifically, he wanted a young woman who would draw in the female audience and serve as a role model for them. William Dozier reached out to editor Julius Schwartz about this idea and Schwartz knew just the men to add to the creative team: artist Carmine Infantino and writer Gardner Fox.

Barbara Gordon, otherwise known as Batgirl, is seen as a particularly feminist character by many fans. Unlike many female versions of male characters, Batgirl did not plan to take on the title. She sewed the Batgirl costume to get a shock out of her father, Commissioner James Gordon, for a policeman's ball she was planning on attending. As previously showcased in Fox's writing, we see a valuing of work that is traditionally feminized when we are shown Barbara sewing her costume. This can be understood as quite empowering for women as they are invited to wonder if they too could sew a costume and potentially become a hero. She proves quite capable of less traditionally feminine work, too, when she saves Bruce Wayne from Killer Moth by just the second page. Fox gives Gordon a Ph.D. from Gotham State University, where she graduated summa cum laude, and with a brown belt in judo.

The first piece of information that we learn about Barbara Gordon in her introductory comic is that she is a librarian. Much like Wonder Woman serving as a secretary, many women worked as librarians, and this job holds additional meaning for Batgirl. While Batman has his own detective methods, Batgirl uses her research skills to sort through files, card catalogs, newspapers, and books. She often exhibits a drive for knowledge that functions in a helping capacity. These methods prove quite effective, leaving even Batman to comment, "We must respect Batgirl's ways and means, Robin! It's enough for us to know she has them!" when Robin expresses a wish to know how she figured out the "tricky scheme" in "The True-False Face of Batman" (39).[33] The panel places Batgirl in the foreground looking quite content and assured while the confused Batman and Robin look diminished in perspective. This visually supports Batman's comment about Batgirl's superiority and authority beyond that of the great detective and his sidekick.

One of the things that is most loved about her is the way in which she decides to be Batgirl for herself. Her motivation is simply self-empowerment through the means of improving her intellectual and physical skills.

In creating Barbara Gordon, Carmine Infantino designed her costume and motorcycle, Julius Schwartz made her Commissioner Gordon's daughter, and it seems likely Fox looked to his sister, Kay, for further inspiration in his writing of the character.

Kay Fox never married and did not appear to have many close friends, but she was well-known in her community. Alan Rumrill, of the Historical Society of Cheshire County, which she was a part of, knew Kay Fox his whole life and stated: "She seemed to have two sides to her personality: the quite serious professional and the outgoing, strong and confident woman—like several of the super-heroes that have become a part of American culture."[34]

The place where she made the largest impact was through her role as the head of the Keene Public Library for twenty-nine years. Intentional or not, she lived her life in a manner that fell in line with the aims of second-wave feminism with its emphasis on finding fulfillment through building a career. Gardner's daughter Lynda adored her. Kay doted on her niece and left her home in Keene to her when she died. It was in this location that Lynda Fox Cohen continued her aunt's work. Obviously, these women made a very positive mark in their community.

Gardner Fox also made a positive mark, and part of that was from his inclusion of strong female characters, even if he made a few missteps in his exploration of feminine strengths and weaknesses. He had written many empowered female characters before, but he may have seen writing Batgirl as an opportunity to examine what a super-hero whose gender is an intended identification point might be like. This proposed exploration often focuses on Batgirl's preoccupation on her appearance, and the peak of this is found in 1968's "Batgirl's Costume Cut-Ups!" which features a cover showcasing a Batgirl who is much more concerned about a run in her tights than Batman and Robin, who aren't doing well in the fight behind her.

Throughout the issue, Batgirl's struggles with being a feminine super-hero are a main theme. This can be seen in these kinds of momentary lapses, each of which she describes as an "instinctive female reaction."[35] She resolves herself to "be a crook-catcher first—and a glance- catcher second," after her femininity exposes her three times. Yet, when she jumps into the fray a fourth time, something slightly different happens. Instead of her femininity being a hindrance, she helps the crime fighters by extending her "shapely leg" to examine the run in her tights thereby catching the criminals' eyes. This distraction allows the heroes to win the fight despite the fact that the odds were three to nine. On the last page of the comic, she states, "My feminine weakness betrayed me so often in the past—I just had to prove it has its strong points too!" The fact that these are the last words of the issue makes it feel like it is the lesson we should learn after reading it.

While it is certainly an attempt to inform readers that women can use their femininity to their advantage, this isn't exactly a strong feminist message, and the fact that the cover contains no hints at the final lesson makes it a bit of a failure. There are significantly more moments like this in Fox's Silver Age work when compared to the stories he wrote in the Golden Age. These moments could have been the influence of the Comics Code Authority's projection of femininity at the time or the impact that editor Julius Schwartz had in comparison to Fox's previous editors like Sheldon Mayer, who edited Wonder Woman.

Regardless, we can still see a pattern of Fox attempting to depict women as he saw them in real life, and that is better than some have done. Additionally, any preoccupation Batgirl may had about her appearance does not take away from the fact that she is an empowered woman, both in and out of costume. Fox's ability to write believable, multi-faceted women was on exhibit again in this era when he got a chance to bring back the first costumed character he wrote for.

The series of issues that make up "Zatanna's Search" form yet another landmark moment in comics history for many reasons. Instead of simply bringing Zatara the Master Magician (from the 1940s–50s Action Comics) into the Silver Age, his mysterious daughter Zatanna leads the way to him. Gardner Fox came up with this twist on the revival pattern in a brainstorm session, and Julius Schwartz approved. Artist and co-creator Murphy Anderson gave Zatanna a top hat and tails, albeit with fishnets instead of suit pants, to capture the look of a stage magician just like her father Zatara. Also like her father, she is an actual magician, who casts her spells by speaking the words backwards in the same way.

She was first introduced in 1964's *Hawkman* #4, kicking off a plot line spread across more than two years and multiple titles in what was the first multi-title crossover event. As she tries to find her missing father, she comes across the likes of Batman, the Atom, Green Lantern, and Elongated Man, all culminating in an issue of *Justice League of America*. Impressively, the entire sequence was written by Fox. The slow reveal must have been fun for fans of the already established magician. This playfulness is seen in the first issue, aptly titled "The Girl Who Split in Two!" where it takes ten pages before it is confirmed that she is Zatara's daughter. Zatanna is split in half due to a misfired spell she cast to try and investigate two possible clues as to the location of her father. The way Fox plays with her speech here is particularly clever as it could be seen as a nod to the puzzling readers might have to do to understand Zatara's backwards spell casting. As she is split in half, we only get half of the words she is speaking. Her speech doesn't become complete until the two halves of her are put back together.

Another reason that these issues with Zatanna are such a fun sequence is the way that Schwartz decided to release them at what seemed random intervals, thereby placing readers in the same position as the hero; each reader had to keep their eyes peeled for the next issue she was in to complete the narrative, making it a quest for fans to find Zatanna at the same time as Zatanna was on a quest to find her father. This type of emphasis on the fun aspects of comics is exemplary of the Silver Age even as DC began to lose some of its sparkle behind the scenes.

Regardless of how many comics DC was able to sell, the late 1960s brought an increased awareness of the industry that had never before existed. This is due in large part to the revivals from the first half of the Silver Age, which galvanized older fans into an organized fandom. They found each other through the addresses attached to submissions in the letter columns and worked together to help the characters they loved succeed; they formed a community out of what was once a largely solitary activity. The main team behind this was Jerry Bails and Roy Thomas, who had been put in touch with each other by Gardner Fox. Bails told Fox that his writing of *All-Star* made Bails the moral person he became, and the physical issues Fox sold him made even more of an impact on Bails. That stack of issues could be described as the true source of fandom. The kindness the three men showed as they bought and lended those issues helped form friendships that lasted many shifts in careers as they each moved in and out of the comic industry in different ways. The arrival of *Alter-Ego* brought with it awards and conventions that put Fox in the spotlight like never before.

A spotlight in the form of the Bat Signal was also shining bright during this time when the *Batman* television series took over family viewing and exposed even more people to Gardner Fox's stories.

Fox wasn't the only one in the family to gain notoriety at this time; his sister, Kay, was honored for Outstanding Library Achievement at the Library Awards in 1961 and may have been the inspiration for Batgirl. This librarian super-hero is considered a feminist icon and she was written when Gardner's daughter was twenty-four, thus potentially giving him an awareness of feminism many of his contemporaries may not have had. Fox had always written strong female characters, and the Silver Age provided him more opportu-nities to continue this pattern. Zatanna's arrival formed the first multi-title crossover event and he also wrote for Star Sapphire, who becomes a much more prominent figure in the *Green Lantern* books he and fellow writer John Broome shared writing duties on. Things were certainly looking good for Fox despite DC's ever-decreasing readership.

His fame was spreading overseas as well, with his literary agent August Lenniger selling translated copies of his novels to places like Norway, Germany, and France.

Unfortunately, Gardner Fox's brush with fame was quickly followed by disappointment. Before the end of the 1960s, he would have to re-evaluate his life in the comic industry.

CHAPTER THIRTEEN

And Defeat

The latter half of the 1960s brought major changes to the comics industry yet again, and Gardner Fox was especially impacted by these shifts. After being a part of so much of DC's success, he learned that this was not being reflected in his treatment by the company. Worse, he discovered that he wasn't the only one. This injustice prompted him and his colleagues to band together in the hopes of receiving their proper dues, however, their attempt ended in calamity.

Now known as the Writers' Strike, this moment can be seen as the end of the Silver Age of comics. After being effectively pushed out of DC, Fox moved to the company's biggest rival where an old friend had found himself working. Fox's time at Marvel was sadly overshadowed by the string of negative events that the Writers' Strike kicked off in Fox's life, leaving him feeling less committed to writing comics regardless of where he was working. Impressively, he was still doing timely work and put his stamp on two of Marvel's big titles. Fox may have seen the last years where he was active in the comic industry as being filled with bitterness, but he still found a way to fit in a few more accomplishments before he left.

The late 1960s was a difficult era for DC, forcing it to make big changes. After the campy Batman phase prompted by the TV show faded, something many creators and editors had originally been looking forward to, comic sales plunged across the whole DC lineup. Making things worse, younger readers were increasingly turning to Marvel. In the minds of upper management, the solution was deemed new leadership.

They didn't look far when choosing Carmine Infantino to turn the company around. In 1967, Infantino was promoted to Editorial Director, making him the first artist to be in that position there. He proceeded to promote other artists to editor positions as he felt the the company needed more visually minded people. They may have lost one of their most popular artists, but Infantino did indeed help to keep DC alive. Disappointingly, this survival did not extend to a group of DC's established writers.

The Writer's Strike started when it was discovered that some writers and artists were getting paid more than others. Fox felt uncomfortable and saw no reason for that to be the case. As news of this imbalance spread, a group of writers decided to form a union of sorts. The group included Bill Finger, Gardner Fox, Arnold Drake, France Herron, and Otto Binder. Their demands were simple: they wanted medical insurance, fair pay, and a pension plan. Most of them had been a part of DC for over 20 years, and DC had acquired the rights to their work, so they felt it was deserved regardless of the fact that this would be considered an unusual request for freelancers.

Gardner's daughter, Lynda, reported feeling morose when she learned what was going on. Despite his years as a lawyer, she knew her father wasn't a good self-advocate. As she predicted, DC president Jack Liebowitz did not approve of these developments. They did get a slight pay raise; however, he began to quietly pass the writers' assignments over to other, mostly younger, writers. Fox wasn't certain what role Infantino had to play in these events, but he felt sure that Infantino never stuck up for the writers. It would be easy for Fox to make him the bad guy, but that isn't who Gardner Fox was. As a matter of fact, in 1984, Fox still considered him his favorite artist to work with thanks to his "special touch."[36]

Regardless of what feelings they might have had for each other, Infantino had to do what Leibowitz wanted him to do. He told Fox that he would no longer be working with Julius Schwartz and would instead work with editor Mort Weisinger, who was notoriously difficult and controlling. That was Fox's last straw. Tactics like these pushed every member of the group to quit. They left feeling disappointed, sad, and bitter. After dedicating a large part of their lives to the comics industry, they were treated as if they didn't matter. Gardner's daughter described him as devastated. Gardner's wife said worse. She felt the writers had been gotten rid of and were treated like trash. These harsh descriptions are supported by a particular event that marks a major turn in his life.

Close to Christmas, in 1968, Gardner Fox suffered a stroke. The night this occurred, he and his wife had gone to a cocktail party at his sister-in-law's house in Greenwich, like they had many times before. It was the end of the night and everybody had begun leaving when someone looked at Gardner and commented on how drunk he seemed to be. This was a red flag to those who knew him well because Gardner drank his pina coladas without the rum. They were lucky enough to have a doctor friend there, and he realized Gardner was having a stroke. His health was never the same after that.

According to his wife, it was "the DC thing" that started it all. His years of cigar smoking certainly contributed as well, but increased stress can and does create the potential for a stroke. It is rather sad and ironic that the demand item he listed most in his explanation of the Writers' Strike was health care.

Thankfully, this scary event wasn't debilitating, and the family was able to pretend like it never happened. Gardner's daughter-in-law, Martha, even had trouble remembering it. As such, Fox's comic career was able to continue, but his drive to write comic books suffered after these events. I argue that the industry, as a whole, changed due to this failed Writers' Strike.

The end of the Silver Age is not clearly defined, with several moments culminating in a shift away from the bright colors and optimism so present in the resurgence of comics that had started in 1956. The inability to point to a definitive ending moment reveals how limited and arbitrary this framework can be. Still, it can be useful shorthand when describing the changes in the industry.

Much like *Showcase* #4 is generally accepted to have officially kicked off the Silver Age, some scholars want to point to a particular narrative as bringing it to a close, such as the story arc where Spider-Man's girlfriend Gwen Stacy would die in 1973, as Arnold T. Blumberg maintains. Others point to the changes in creators. For instance, Craig Shutt claims that the combination of Jack Kirby's move to DC and Mort Weisinger's retirement marks the end. Both of these occurred in 1970.

If we are going to use creative changes as the primary lens, the little known Writers' Strike would be far more qualifying. I assert that the end of the Silver Age occurred when DC lost Gardner Fox, Bill Finger, France Herron, Arnold Drake, John Broome, and Otto Binder in 1968.[37] DC had to replace their established greats with a new team of creators, and the company was never the same.

There were certainly successful comics after this moment, but the torch had effectively been passed to a new generation. This perception is something that Fox seemed to share, and it came up when he was spotlighted at a New York convention.

Fox's comments at 1971's New York Comic Art Convention suggest a strong shift in how he felt about the comics industry at that time. Both he and artist/writer Jim Steranko were made guests of honor, with publisher James Warren giving the keynote address. As a guest of honor, he was treated to an awards luncheon where he sat down for an interview with convention organizer Phil Seuling. The first question Seuling asked was how many words Fox thought he had written so far. As Fox did keep track of these things, his staggering estimation that he had written close to fifty million words is hard to deny.[38]

The interview covered many topics specific to a guest of honor such as what his sources were and what he found rewarding. Fox displayed how modest and courteous he was, responding with things like the dinner being rewarding enough and admitting that he sometimes just had to do the best he could under deadlines. A later question from the audience got a surprising answer. The person asked about how to break into the industry and, while Fox did go on to provide some solid advice, he started by saying, "I'll make this a truthful answer. If I were a young writer today, I would write for anything but comics." He went on to explain that this advice was based on the Academy of Comic Book Arts reporting that sales weren't very good, and it would be better to write for television because it was going to last; however, one cannot help but read some of Fox's resignation into this response.

Roy Thomas also wrote up a brief biography in celebration of Fox for the event. Opening with the question of how to cover Fox's career in only 700 words, Thomas hits on many high- lights starting before the release of Superman to where Fox's career was at that moment stating," Today, after more than a third of a century of legend-birthing, of helping to create the shorthand mythology of several generations, a slowing down would seem to be called for..." (2).[39]

Even though this praise is as true as it is grand, the ending sentiment seems to be all Fox could hear. Thomas even ended his piece, much like the biography written for him from the 1965 comic convention, with information about what was coming out next for Fox. To no avail. Fox left feeling "like an old horse being put out to pasture after all these years."[40] Fox would later say that he simply lost interest in comics and wanted to focus more on writing novels, but it is pretty clear that he was experiencing some complicated emotions regarding the industry at this point in his life. In contrast to this, some big names in the comic industry would soon make it clear just how wanted he remained.

While Gardner Fox was searching for justice at DC, Roy Thomas had been busy carving his own path in the industry and found a way to make good on an old promise. Thomas had moved to New York City to work at DC under Mort Weisinger in 1965. As many others did, Thomas found him difficult to work with. Things would change for the better after he wrote Stan Lee a letter praising his work and expressing a desire to buy him a drink at some point. Lucky for Thomas, Lee remembered him and invited Thomas to take a writer's test. He passed and was hired as a staff writer. Not long after, Thomas proved himself to be far more valuable as an editor by virtue of his impressive comics knowledge.

According to Fox, it was Stan Lee who suggested to Thomas that he might like to work for them; however, Thomas had needed no prodding. As a long-time fan who wanted to repay Fox's kindness, he was more than happy to bring Fox on board. As Thomas described it, "We were never close friends or anything, but I made sure he had work at Marvel after he was pushed out at DC."[41]

One of the first projects Gardner Fox took on during his time at Marvel was writing a character Thomas had co-created called Red Wolf.

The western genre largely faded out when super-heroes took over the top selling list again; however, Gardner Fox never fully stopped writing them. In 1961, he co-created the first western super-hero, a Native American warrior called Super-Chief with Carmine Infantino, and he got the chance to write a similar first during his time at Marvel. Working with artist Syd Shores, Fox wrote for Red Wolf when he was made the first Native American Marvel super-hero to carry his own title. This newer Red Wolf was transformed into an orphaned Cheyenne who was raised by a family of white colonizers and named Johnny Wakely.

Fox's humanitarian drive meshed with Marvel's quite well in that this hero starts out both a brother to, and protector of, all men regardless of their color. Along with this kind of morality, we also get a mix of standard western villains alongside villains similar to the ones seen in Fox's Ghost Rider, such as Koumt'ou Kia, a demon rider of the plains.

It proved a short run, but it is remembered for its originality and its status as one of the last of the "true" western comics.[42] This trueness might be up for debate, but one can certainly agree that Fox did include many of the classic clichés that fans of the genre enjoy, such as the way that Red Wolf, and the generations of Owayo Ata'hae warriors before him, are personified by the land itself, and it is the land that he draws on to gain strength and the justification for his actions. These types of considerations were common in Fox's work in the western genre and it may have been because of his father's influence.

Gardner may have seen his westerns as an opportunity to honor his father and share the wilderness skills Leon Fox taught him. For as moneyed and educated as Leon was, his roots were in the country. He would later return to these roots. After Fox's mother died in Bellows Falls, Vermont, on February 3, 1967, Leon moved to a house in Alstead, New Hampshire. Always keeping his eye on the beautiful, the house was located about a quarter mile down the road from the gorgeous spring-fed Vilas Pool. There, he had a stream and a small pond that ran through his yard where he could catch trout. He also had a garden and a chicken coop, showing a strong sense of self-reliance even in his older years.

Gardner and his father, Leon Fox. (Courtesy of Theresa Fox)

One of daughter Lynda's favorite stories was when she and her brother Jeffery were visiting "Pop," and he took them out to the barn to kill a chicken for dinner. Jeffrey was unable to go through with it, but Lynda wasn't so squeamish. Her nephew, Greg, believes that his aunt and great grandfather were both "very pleased with her killer instinct."[43] I'm sure that dinner tasted a lot better for the two of them at least.

Gardner Fox showed a similar preference for a life outside the pressures of modern society and this comes through in his westerns. Even though Leon was in his mid-eighties by this point, he remained able to take care of himself and his land quite well. This extended beyond what many people might expect. When he saw some men putting up telephone poles in front of his house, he knew they were doing it incorrectly, so he went outside to supervise. The workers assumed he was some crazy over-controlling old man until he started to get technical in his criticism revealing his experience as an electrical engineer. He was sharp well into old age.

A year shy of 90, Leon Fox died on February 25, 1973, leaving Gardner with no living parents. It is hard to say how this impacted him as it was something else he didn't talk about. As a result, Greg Fox only has a vague recollection of his great-grandfather's death: "The Foxes are stoic, to say the least."[44] This matches well with stereotypes often seen in the western genre. That wasn't the only genre Fox wrote in at Marvel, and the other genres contained heroes who were much more vocal and emotive.

Shortly after Fox started writing Red Wolf, he was given a chance to write for a certain sorcerer supreme. Having co-created Doctor Fate, Fox was an excellent choice (by Roy Thomas) to put on Doctor Strange, and he quickly brought in the same Lovecraftian aesthetics that worked so well for his previous magical doctor. This was a change of pace for the character, but Marvel had also been adapting stories from *Weird Tales,* where horror writer H.P. Lovecraft published most of his tales, making it fit in with the company's branding at the time.

The only problem is that the Lovecraft estate stayed highly protective of the Cthulhu Mythos. Marvel was able to get around it due to an already established agreement with the Robert E. Howard Estate, which got them Conan as well. The chosen Lovecraftian monster was Shuma-Gorath, from a Howard story titled "The Curse of the Golden Skull." As the creature was really nothing more than a name in that tale, Marvel remained free to do what it wanted with it. Still, this is why the phrase "featuring concepts created by Robert E. Howard" was included on the title pages of the issues where Fox sets the stage for the grand reveal that Steve Englehart later delivers on.

This isn't to say that Fox, a long-time fan and emulator of Lovecraft, didn't deliver on the incorporation of the mythos. The Shambler of the Sea was very Cthulhuesque as an unmentionable green and tentacled monster who slept for uncounted eons until the day he rose from the sea. Fox also brought in a reptilian horror named the Sligguth, complete with chanting minions. This comfort largely stemmed from his prior work on Doctor Fate.

The easiest comparison to make is to Doctor Fate. Doctor Strange has more weaknesses than the previous doctor, but they do have a lot in common. Fox even makes their speech patterns similar with lots of archaic language that he came across in his occult research.

This use of horror and the occult was something that had not been possible for the major comic companies since the creation of the Comics Code Authority.

Around the time that Fox switched over to writing for Marvel, the Comics Code Authority relaxed some of its rules, making horror comics a viable genre again. After testing the waters with the vampire Morbius, Stan Lee hastened to release a full line of horror comics featuring classical monsters. The most popular of these was *Tomb of Dracula,* which came out in 1972.

As popular as it became, the series had a rough start. Having already been written by multiple creators, Fox was given the opportunity to write issues #5 and #6. Many of Fox's works had horror elements in them, and he had even written some EC horror comics before, making this a good fit. Fox was able to work in his knowledge of tracking and the occult as well as his love of archaic language. Much like he did for Doctor Strange, he also introduced Lovecraftian themes. The biggest impact Fox had on the series was his introduction of a romance between Rachel Van Helsing and Frank Drake. This relationship would remain throughout the rest of the series.

Still, now-editor Roy Thomas felt that Fox's take didn't click.[45] Fox did better with the one-off black-and-white horror comics that Marvel was putting out, such as those in *Vampire Tales* #1 and #2. The story from the first issue, titled "Revenge of the Unliving," released in 1973, showed Fox playing with the vampire mythos once again as his protagonist is able to doubt the existence of vampires due to their turning into dust when they die. The art proved a downfall for "Five Claws to Tryphon" after artist Jesus Blasco ran into deadline issues. John Romita ended up finishing the last four pages and the two styles didn't mesh as well as they could have. Regardless, the Peruvian-based story is classic Fox, complete with a man who rises to the status of a hero by saving an attractive woman he meets by entering into another dimension. One of the reasons that the story stands out is the extra-dimensional vampire Typhon, who proves a fascinating entry into the vampire canon, which had become more fixed by that time. He was closer to an eldritch horror who happens to drink the blood of his prisoners and has a weakness to light because he was born of darkness.

It was these black-and-white horror books, which also gave his old friend a chance to write a John Carter of Mars-influenced feature titled "World of Warlocks" in *Monsters Unleashed*, that Thomas reports he would have kept Fox busy on, "if nothing else."[46]

In the end, it was Fox, not Marvel, who put an end to this brief chapter of his life. He just never felt at ease working for Marvel. How different Marvel's scripting method was didn't help the situation. Working there, he was required to write the plot synopsis and then go back and dialog the art when finished. Fox had done a lot of work for a lot of companies, but the way Marvel did things seemed backwards to him. He decided it was better to retire from comics and focus on writing his novels instead.

Gardner Fox experienced some challenging times near the end of his comics career. While the Writer's Strike may have cemented the bond he had with his fellow strikers, Bill Finger, Otto Binder, and Arnold Drake, the event had taken a toll on him and likely contributed to his stroke. Bad things often come in threes and he would lose both his parents within a handful of years later. Thankfully, Fox was able to withstand these tribulations. After a brief stint at Marvel, Fox made the decision to write his thought-provoking stories on his own terms by giving up his comic work in favor of becoming a retired novelist. He more than deserved his slowing down.

PART SIX

During these years of writing, the idea of a barbarian-swordsman of my own ran through my mind. He must be a man fit to stand beside those other heroes and (I hoped) to rival their valiant deeds. It was not until the summer of 1968, however, that I got the chance I had long been waiting for.

—Gardner Fox[1]

CHAPTER FOURTEEN

Fox Finally Finds His Freedom

After the stress leading to his departure from the comic industry, Gardner Fox's retirement allowed him to follow his passions, which, in large part, brought him back to the things he loved as a youth. This consisted of novels and games in the sword-and-sorcery genre. Both of these would end up financing his later years. He had remained financially comfortable during his years writing comics due to a pay rate increase of around $14 dollars more than when he started, but he could make about the same amount of money, or more, writing novels. An added benefit was that removing comics from the equation freed up about two thirds of his time. Any missing income was supplemented by his prior works being reprinted.

Not that making a huge amount of money was particularly important to him. In the interview with Phil Seuling at the 1971 Comic Art Convention, Fox was asked what he would be doing if a guardian angel came along with millions of dollars and told him he could write whatever he wanted, and Fox responded by saying he enjoyed writing the sword-and-sorcery novels he was already doing, adding that the money wouldn't change his life beyond giving him a sense of security.[2]

Evidently, Fox's sense of fulfillment stayed high during these later years. A lot of his fantasy novels can be described as imitative potboilers, but the genre thrives in its slight variations and this is something Fox seemed to be aware of. Nonetheless, he didn't just spend all his time banging out novels on the typewriter.

Gardner and his wife Lynda moved to New Jersey to be closer to his family and he got about as close as he could to retirement. Just when he finally learned how to relax, his love of comics returned. Fox saw the the comics industry shift one more time in his life when he became aware of the expansion of smaller independent publishers in the 1980s. Fox was encouraged to jump back in the fray by a new friend, and this book could have had a very different ending had Fox not died before his final story came to fruition.

Gardner's retirement included a lot of work, but it was on his terms and based around the things he loved most.

Just one year after Fox left DC, he kicked off a string of sword-and-sorcery novels starting with his barbarian character named Kothar. The character was first conceived when Fox read Edgar Rice Burroughs' *Gods of Mars* on his eleventh birthday. He had tried to bring some of that desire for a Burroughsesque adventure into his comic book writing; Cotton Carver and Adam Strange are two examples of this, but the summer of 1968 would bring him the chance to see it fully realized. This is when the publisher of Belmont Books, Harry Shorten, offered him the opportunity to "put flesh and blood around my nebulous idea of this barbarian swordsman" as Fox put it in the fanzine *Star-Studded Comics* #17's "Behind the Swords." Fox continued, "He was anxious to establish a fantasy hero for his Belmont line and I was more than anxious, I was literally tickled pink at the chance."[1]

In creating this hero, Fox's subconscious was hard at work. Kothar's name was only one letter transposed from his previous muscular hero appearing in "Engine of the Gods," from 1946's *Planet Stories*, named Kortha. Fox had no recollection of this until a fan named Larry Herndon, of *Star-Studded Comics*, mentioned it.

One of the things Fox wanted most was for Kothar to have a special and individualized sword. This desire materialized through Frostfire, a magical sword given to Kothar from the wizard Afgorkon, who just happens to have been dead for fifty thousand years. Regardless of his first inspiration point, it is clear that Robert E. Howard's Conan formed a main influence. The similarities are mostly in the overall plot structure, but there are also surface-level nods such as the fact that Conan is Cimmerian while Kothar is Cumberian.

There are some changes, though. Along with increased stakes and intensity, there is a hidden intelligence within the story structure in which this not-so-intelligent hero is placed. This is displayed in the first book of the series, *Kothar: Barbarian Swordsman* (1969), with a mythic narrative complete with a name drop of Ulysses and a labyrinth full of different kinds of traps. As much as it can be seen as falling into the Greek tradition, it also takes on Arthurian aspects. Both forms often show a hero rejecting various temptations as he moves from one battle to the next.

Despite all this, Kothar is not a traditional hero. He is a sellsword, or a sword for hire, even when he does take on a heroic quest. The sword itself is what keeps him on the straight and narrow due to the fact that it cannot be owned by someone with wealth. Anytime he accrues too much wealth, it gets taken away in various different ways; thus, he is always questing and falling into heroics. While the paperback novel is most certainly a potboiler, it has its rousing moments.

Another major fantasy character Fox created in his later years is Kyrik. Fox's work can be seen as rather imitative, but many of the genres he wrote in thrive because of their known conventions. It is in the slight variations that readers find reason to read them. Knowing these conventions, then, becomes important as each writer must build off of what has come before. One can see from where Fox drew inspiration as well as who was inspired by him. Further, we can see how he was inspired by himself as he continued writing what had worked in his previous stories.

Reading through the first Kyrik novel, *Kyrik: Warlock Warrior* (1975), it was easy to draw comparisons between it and *Kothar: Barbarian Swordsman*. Magic is equally important, but Kothar relies on other people's magic, whilst Kyrik is a wizard himself. Just as Kothar is defined by Frostfire, Kyrik is defined by Devadonides, who had been king before Kyrik overthrew him. Kothar has one main love interest, who objectifies the hero as much as he objectifies her, while Kyrik has two, along with a worshipful relationship with a demoness.

The main difference is the way in which these first books from each series are inverses of each other. Fox's writing of Kothar explores what the start of a hero's journey looks like, and what those narratives contain, whereas Krylik explores the end of a hero's journey, and how a lifetime of heroics impacts the character behind them. It is also worth recognizing that Kothar can be read as a series of smaller adventures in comparison to Kyrik's exciting, unified storyline. Basically, Kyrik is everything Kothar is and more.

From this perspective, it might seem as if Fox simply copied and expanded his prior story structure; however, running *Kothar: Barbarian Swordsman* and *Kyrik: Warlock Warrior* through a data-mining tool reveals more nuances. Work in the digital humanities includes the use of different kinds of technological tools, which are software and applications that aid in the gathering, filtering, or presenting of research. The specific tool I used for my textual analysis is Voyant, a web-based tool designed to facilitate interpretation via word frequency distribution lists that can be visualized as word clouds, trend charts, etc. Voyant reveals Kothar as defined most by who he is as a Cumberian and, even more importantly, a barbarian. His name is used often, but not nearly as much as Kyrick's. The more established hero is defined mostly by his antagonist, Devadonides, and his main love interest, Aryalla. His name is used more often because he has a stronger cast of characters he interacts with and he has already gained notoriety from his historic adventures.

I expected to see some of the more obvious parallels, such as their often-described grey or black horses, but terms like "man," "eyes," and "hand" emerge with much more frequency.[3] This helps elucidate the way in which Fox uses these heroes to examine masculinity as a context for how they see the world, how others see them, and what they physically do as a result of those perceptions. There is only a slight difference between the action-based men, but Kyrik is shown to be more observational in comparison to the more inexperienced Kothar.

Pairing the two novels in this way clarifies just how much actually changes when one starts as a hero instead of becoming one and highlights the differences between these seemingly similar novels.

While we don't know if he ever picked up *Dungeons & Dragons*, Fox's sword-and-sorcery writing made its way into the game and he did participate in the related game industry. *Dungeons & Dragons* is a fantasy-based tabletop role-playing game that first came out in 1974. In it, players create their characters and embark on imaginary adventures where they defeat enemies, gather treasure, and the like, with the specific goal of leveling up through the earning of experience points. Led by a dungeon master, this all takes place in the same world, which was created by Gary Gygax and Dave Arneson. That world is described in booklets detailing various options including character types, dungeons, and more. Gygax was a fan of Gardner Fox and he got the idea for a powerful undead sorcerer called a lich from the living-dead wizard Afgorkon, who gives Kothar his magical sword.

The connection doesn't stop there. Two years later, a magazine titled *The Dragon* came out. This official *Dungeons & Dragons* magazine, put out by Tactical Studies Rules (TSR), much like the game, contains supplemental source materials as well as stories designed to inspire. Fox regularly contributed. Within the pages of this magazine, Fox told the tales of Niall of the Far Travels, whose first appearance was in *The Dragon* #2, and he would re-appear multiple times. The stories start out much like Kothar tales with named swords, giant serpents, explorations of bodily control, and empowered women who are either evil or protective of Naill—sometimes both. His work for TSR opened other doors as well.

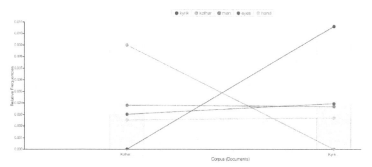

Word Frequency Chart for Kothar: Barbarian Swordsman *and* Kyrik: Warlock Warrior *via Voyant*

Fox played many games and took the hobby seriously, even creating a game himself. His family remembers playing 1981's *Dark Tower* with him, so he was at least familiar with how these types of fantasy games could function. This would have helped him when he turned to making one of his own.

Titled *Warlocks and Warriors*, players are tasked with escorting a princess from a seaport to her father's castle. The reward is half the kingdom. Considering the escort mission, locations, and character options, it is recognizable as part of the Fox canon. As such, the playing of it allows one to step inside a Fox-style sword-and-sorcery narrative. The one major critique is the lack of initiative for the princess pawn. Fox's stories paint the women his heroes rescue as fairly capable and intelligent on her own, but there is no opportunity for the game to show that. The way the princess pawn is passed back and forth as a result of duels is problematic, as it turns the only female pawn into nothing more than an object necessary for the winning of the game. That said, this mechanic is rewarding and adds to the fun of the game.

The ease with which the player can narrativize the game play is also striking. As one moves from location to location, the results of the die roll inform the way the player views their effectiveness as a warlock or warrior.

Even to those unaware of who Gardner Fox was, it must have been obvious that the game was created by a writer. Indeed, it was advertised in TSR's catalogs as part of their "famous authors" series along with Fritz Leiber's *Lankhmar* and L. Sprague de Camp's *Cohorts: Game of Roman Checkers*.

Fox was no longer actively writing comics, but that didn't stop fans from reading his work and discovering who he was.

In 1980, Roy Thomas wrote Gardner Fox asking to use Gardner-Fox-the-character. Fox gave his permission with a request that a copy be sent to him so that he could show his grand-children. He thought they would "get a big laugh out of it!!!"[4] I'm sure they did get a laugh out of it when Fox showed up as an actual fox in the memorable *Captain Carrot and His Amazing Zoo Crew!* #14 a few years later.

Additionally, an early supporter of creator rights, and the first female president of DC, Jenette Kahn enacted a policy enabling Fox to receive residuals when DC reprinted his works in its giant-size issues. These reprints helped maintain his fan base.

Interactions with these fans would sometimes result in amusing stories. In contrast to his fans, who were often long-haired "hippies," Gardner's wife, Lynda, was a proper and conservative woman. Her grandchildren would find this dis-junction arriving at their door in Yonkers hilarious. Outside of a few key moments, the quiet Gardner seldom talked with his grandchildren about his work; therefore, the idea of fans coming over to speak with him in this manner was even funnier to them.

Overall, he had a lot of respect for his fans and would invite them in during his retirement years, even if their adulation made him uncomfortable. Some would go as far as to declare that Fox "built DC comics," but he would never make such claims.[5].... He preferred to have an intellectual discussion about his work with fans who were passionate and knowledge-able about it, such as those he had with early comic scholars Jerry Bails and Roy Thomas.

As shocked as the elder Lynda might have been, Gardner was surprised. Even knowing comics fandom existed, he could not have been prepared for it to grow to such an extent. This was something no creator was prepared for. After all, comics were seen as a throw-away culture when Fox first started. While he believed they are a legitimate art form, the idea of getting an award for it was something he proved ill prepared for.

Still, he had four or five plaques on the wall, the big tall Jules Verne Award for Life-time Achievement from Skycon II, and an Alley award displayed in his bedroom and office. Fox felt proud of these, but he remained a modest man and would become almost bashful when someone would bring them up. Perhaps his most significant award is the Inkpot Award he picked up at the San Diego Comic-Con in 1978. He was also made one of the honorees in DC Comics' 50th anniversary *Fifty Who Made DC Great*. Impressively, Gardner wasn't the only Fox winning awards at the time.

His sister, Kay Fox, was leading quite the successful life as well. In addition to being honored for Outstanding Library

Achievement, she received the Granite State Award for Outstanding Public Service from Keene State College in 1973. She stayed a busy woman with a list of accomplishments and activities too large to list here. Showing just how much she

Kay Fox breaks ground on the Keen Public Library addition (Curtesy of the Keene Sentinel)

had in common with her brother, she served as editor of the *Published History of Keene* and became president of Monadnock Region Humane Society.

Of all the ways she positively impacted her community, it was her work though the library that is most remarkable. In *Our Window to a Wider World: An Informal History of Keen Public Library,* Susan M. Peery states that the hiring of Kay Fox, during the early 1950s, was itself a major accomplishment.[6] As a librarian, she increased accessibility by creating a stronger audio-visual collection and helped with the collection and preservation of history by starting the microfilming of two local newspapers.

Kay went on to become the library director, and, in this role, she expanded the children's department, brought in guest speakers to explore key issues, and wrote a weekly column on noteworthy books and libraries for the *Keene Sentinel.* All her hard work earned her the chance to break ground on a new expansion that would allow the library to swell with 80,000 books being read by 19,000 borrowers.[7] A meeting room in the library was even named in her honor. When she died on

Gardner and Lynda Fox at their son's graduation. (Courtesy of Theresa Fox)

October 6, 1993, her niece Lynda inherited her home and carried on with some of the work Kay started.

Lynda Fox Cohen proved the perfect person to carry on the work of her aunt, and she was an accomplished woman herself. Gardner's daughter graduated from the Ursuline School, an all-girls Roman Catholic school in New Rochelle, New York, before attending Georgetown University. Over the course of her life, she worked in merchandising, advertising, and public relations. Like her aunt and father, she was also a particularly zealous reader. This passion led her to her own form of humanitarian service: teaching illiterate ex-convicts to read. Gardner Fox must have been so proud of his little trouble-maker. Not that she stopped encouraging a little mischief. Passing on the knowledge she gained by testing her boundaries at home, she once pulled her nephew Greg aside to make sure he understood he should go to his grandfather if he ever wanted something because Gardner was the "softee" in comparison to grandma.[8]

When she and her husband moved to Keene in 1993, she continued her aunt's exploration of their family genealogy and, later, posthumously promoted her father by reaching out to people in the comic industry and sharing information about him. She was also active in the Keene Yankee Bottle Club her aunt helped found. As proud as Gardner must have felt when thinking about how his daughter turned out, he was equally proud of his son for different reasons.

Jeffrey Fox's aspirations seem similar to his father's, but he fulfilled them in his own way. He received a bachelor's degree from the Roman Catholic, liberal arts-focused Manhattan College in the Bronx. He followed it with a Master's in Accounting, and, with his cousin Robert Kar graduating from Manhattan College on the same day, his 1978 graduation was attended by a large part of his family. With two graduates, they had the perfect excuse for a festive family party.

That following fall, Jeffrey enlisted in the army. He wanted to perform his civic duty before he started a career. The day he went off to boot camp was the day President Kennedy was assassinated. This caused him a fair amount of stress because he worried he would then have to go to war. Thankfully, because of his degree, that was unlikely to happen. He did his two years working as an accountant for the army and believed himself to be better disciplined for it. Gardner Fox must have been especially proud of his son for being able to do what he couldn't.

Back at home, Jeffrey worked for the New Jersey Department of Education. Additionally, while the younger Lynda remained content to be a "dog mom," her brother gave Gardner Fox grandchildren. With Martha Fox, he had two sons named Greg and Kenneth as well as two daughters named Deborah and Theresa. It is Kenneth who brings to light yet another form of writing Gardner Fox practiced. On his father's online obituary, he stated his best memories were their "long road trips in the old wagon" and when the family would all sing together.[9] There was one song in particular the Fox family sang and it wasn't the same version the rest of the world is familiar with.

Originally penned by Harry McClintock in 1928, "Big Rock Candy Mountain" is a folk song detailing a homeless person's idea of heaven. Many people believe the song speaks to the need to put a positive spin on how likely it is for a homeless person to die during the winter, but this context is only implied in the song. Expanding on the mention of the coming fall, from which this implication stems, Gardner Fox draws a drearier picture with the story being sung on an already bleak November day. More importantly, Fox turns the song into an act of kindness by changing the setting and adding a new character. Instead of a single man walking up on a campfire and telling the tale to those surrounding it, we now get an intimate moment between a dying man and his comrade. Having said that, Gardner always laughed at the part where the person suffering from homelessness dreams of never having to change his socks or take a bath, and it was this he calls back to at the end of his version of the song, thereby keeping the overall tone of the original. This is the part Greg still remembers, even though the tradition of singing it ended in the 1980s.

All of the family events held at Gardner and Lynda's home in Yonkers ended with two after-dinner traditions: a family game of penny-ante Michigan rummy and singing a few songs together including Gardner's version of "Big Candy Rock Mountain," although they never named it as such. In fact, the Fox grandchildren had no idea the song had origins

BESIDE A WESTERN WATERTOWER, ON A
   BLEAK NOVEMBER DAY
ON THE FLOOR OF AN EMPTY BOXCAR,
   A DYING HOBO LAY

HIS COMRADE KNELT BESIDE HIM, WITH
   LOW AND BENDED HEAD
A LISTENING TO THE LAST WORDS THE
   DYING HOBO SAID.

"I'M GOING," SAID THE HOBO, "TO A
   LAND THAT'S FAIR AND BRIGHT
"WHERE YOU NEVER HAVE TO TAKE A
   BATH OR CHANGE YOUR SOCKS AT
   NIGHT --
"WHERE LITTLE STREAMS OF WHISKEY
   COME TRICKLIN' DOWN THE ROCKS
"AND YOU NEVER HAVE TO TAKE A
   BATH OR EVEN CHANGE YOUR SOCKS."

THE HOBO CLOSED HIS EYES AT LAST, AND
   BREATHED HIS LAST REFRAIN.
HIS COMRADE SWIPED HIS SHOES AND
   SOCKS, AND BOARDED AN
   OUTBOUND TRAIN.

        — THE DYING HOBO

*Gardner Fox's "Big Candy Mountain" lyrical
additions. (Courtesy of Theresa Fox)*

beyond Gardner's pen. This train of thought was encouraged after Jeffrey died and his wife gave their daughter, Theresa, the "original lyrics."[10] Both Greg and Theresa were shocked when they heard it outside their family for the first time. These types of traditions were significant within the Fox family and it helped to keep them close. In their later years, Gardner and Lynda decided they wanted to be physically closer, too.

After 39 years in Yonkers, Fox and his wife moved to Cranbury, New Jersey, in order to be closer to their grandchildren. They lived in a senior community named Rossmoor. Fox described it as lovely in a letter he wrote to Roy Thomas dated October 27, 1980.[11] Being closer meant Gardner could do things like attend Grandparents' Day at Theresa's school, and go see the cartoon version of *The Lord of the Rings* with Greg. This would inspire his grandson's love of J.R.R. Tolkien, although Greg wouldn't become the avid reader his grandfather hoped for until after the latter's death. In addition to doing things with his grandchildren, he also found the time to bond with his son over sports. They both supported the Mets and the New York Giants. Showing the love he still had for his alma mater, Gardner also had season tickets for St. John's basketball games. His wife would sometimes join him and once forced an introduction between Gardner and the coach, Lou Carnesecca. The reserved Gardner didn't want to bother him and this moment shows how much his wife's more assertive temperament made for a good counter-balance to his own.

The couple made themselves a part of the local Rossmoor community as well. Unsurprisingly, it was their love of bridge that provided an entry point. They attended many parties and played in a few different groups.

At 69, he finally considered himself retired. Although he still wrote about a novel a year, he was also making time for more recreation. For Fox, this meant time to paint his pewter soldiers, try his hand at gardening, watch more television, and formally pick up birdwatching. The one activity that never changed was spending quality time reading in his chair. His constant drive to learn something new always kept a variety of newspapers, novels, and even fanzines close by.

Even though Gardner Fox considered himself retired from

the comic industry, he never fully separated from it. His main connection to that world continued to be through comic fanzines. He would read them to keep up on business news, but he would also contribute to their letter columns and do interviews. His primary sources were *Mediascene* and *Batmania*, of which Jim Steranko and Richard H. Morrissey, respectively, provided him complimentary copies. This is where he learned Carmine Infantino and Jack Liebowitz were no longer a part of DC. Being rebuffed by the company itself didn't change how he felt about his friends remaining within it, but Fox was still hurt, and this affected his work at Marvel. He seemed certain the comics part of his writing career was over. He still struggled with some of these emotions in 1976. In an interview with Richard H. Morrissey for *YZNGATZ* #3, he said:

> Am I bitter? Who knows? Not really, not any more, anyhow. They were always preaching loyalty at National, but it was always a one-sided loyalty, you had to be loyal to them, but they had no interest in you except for the amount of work you could turn out.[12]

It would be easy to see how a lack of creator's rights would make him feel this way. Fox left feeling unappreciated after all the years he gave DC. Surprisingly, he would soon meet a man at a gaming convention who would not only appreciate him, but get him back into the comics word.

Timothy Truman went to GenCon X, in 1977, because he was working with TSR on the *Dungeons & Dragons* games. The convention mainly focused on *Dungeons & Dragons*, but other table-top games were featured as well. This included Gardner Fox's *Warlocks & Warriors*. Truman was walking around and spotted Fox and his wife sitting out in a hall by themselves. Nobody really knew who Fox was at the event. They looked dapper and friendly, so Truman went over to say hello. He was excited when he realized with whom he was talking. *Kothar: Barbarian Swordsman* had been the first paperback book Truman had purchased. The joy it gave him turned him into a fan of the genre and set him on his path to becoming a fantasy illustrator.

This would have resonated strongly with Fox, who was inspired to write after reading Edgar Rice Burroughs as a youth.

The two men started a friendship and they began exchanging mail. Truman got to know Fox fairly well and described him as "one of the most wonderful people I'd ever met."[13]

Around the time Truman went to the convention, he had just started working for the small comics company Eclipse and informed Fox of the changes that were occurring in the industry in regard to creator's rights.

Fox had worked for both big and small publishers throughout his career in comics, but Eclipse was different in that it allowed creators to own the material they produced. Arriving on the scene in 1977, Eclipse was one of the earliest of the several independent publishers springing up at the time. Dean Mullaney created the company using the knowledge he gained from publishing fanzines and it is best known for publishing the first graphic novel to be sold in a store dedicated specifically to comic books. These independent publishers became the home for many creators who had become dissatisfied by the editorial restrictions in place at the bigger publishing companies like DC and Marvel. Eclipse drew many big names like artist Marshall Rogers and writer Jim Starlin. These creators were just as frustrated as Fox was when he took part in the Writer's Strike.

If Fox had any reservations about coming back to the comic industry, the fact that he was finally getting paid residuals for his work at DC would have helped convince him.

Eclipse seemed like the perfect place for him to dip his toe back into the pool and Timothy Truman did indeed persuade Fox to come out of retirement. Excited, Fox quickly wrote a Kothar-inspired comic titled "The Saving of Sayera" for 1985's *Killer...Tales* by Timothy Truman, featuring a new hero named Daral the Swordsman. Truman was overjoyed.

Gardner must have also enjoyed himself, because he continued writing for Eclipse with 1985's "Wish Upon a Jewel," in *Alien Encounters* #4, being the last Fox-written published comic I could find. It is described as an all-star issue with a cover by John Bolton and other works by Timothy Truman, Tim Conrad, and Mr. Monster, also known as Michael T. Gilbert, who would later go on to publish work on the Gardner Fox collected papers.

"Wish upon a Jewel" is a classic poetic justice tale with a selfish misogynistic protagonist who runs out of gas right around the same time as he spots a new planet. He makes the decision to descend, regardless of the risk that he would not be able to leave, on the chance he would get a promotion. He names the planet after himself before he lands. Fox was of the opinion that the people who would be doing any space-traveling in the future would be tough guys with a western frontier mindset, and one can easily see that kind of manifest destiny-like train of thought exemplified in this lead. Rarely does it get depicted so brutally in Fox's work. The protagonist feels the opposite of many of his previous heroes. Part of this may be a result of what he characterized as a mellowing.

These later years gave Fox more time to read and he began going over his old favorites. He described these books as being filled with treasured friends, including the antagonists. Instead of hating the villains for their dastardly deeds and Machiavellian moves, as he had before, Fox found himself appreciating them with an indulgent smile at the same time he was appropriately shaming their behavior.[14] This can be seen in his sword-and-sorcery work as the villains are given ample attention and the heroes consider morally questionable things. It is on display in "Wish upon a Jewel" as well. The story provides us a protagonist who does some shockingly terrible things; however, he gives himself what he deserves for these actions after finding an orb that grants wishes. Fox's writing of this issue displays a desire to continue writing comics and, if he had lived longer, he might have made a full leap back into DC's pool of writers.

During a phone call, Timothy Truman asked Fox what story he would want to do if he officially came back to comics, and his answer will forever leave his fans dreaming of what could have been.

Fox had previously stated he was running out of ideas when it came to writing Adam Strange, but he apparently had a few more left in him for his second favorite character: the Silver Age Hawkman. After taking some time to think, Fox told Truman he wanted to do a Hawkman story set on Thanagar with a heavy Edgar Rice Burroughs influence. He was thinking of almost a John Carter of Mars type version of Hawkman.

Fox must have been especially excited about this, because his grandson Greg remembered him talking about a project he was considering around this time.

Truman thought it was a great idea, but he was too busy by the time Fox had an answer to his question. When things cleared up for him, he sat down to write Fox a letter saying they would hit up DC and see if they would be interested.

Truman was visiting his parents at the time, so he decided to put the letter in his suitcase and mail it when he got home. Upon his arrival he got a call from Lynda Fox, informing him that her husband had passed away. Gardner had died the very night, and at the very hour, that Truman was writing the letter.

Gardner Fox's death, in 1986, was a surprise, and his whole community mourned.

At 75, he was a healthy and active man, who did the *New York Times* crossword puzzle every day and believed in staying independent just like his father. Then, in December, he came down with pneumonia. He stayed in the hospital for a few days and was doing better before things took a sudden turn for the worse. He died immediately. Adding to the pain, that night was Christmas Eve. His wife was devastated. Showing how important Fox's faith was to him, all the arrangements

In Loving Memory of

Gardner F. Fox

1911-1986

RESURRECTION PRAYER

MOST merciful Father, we commend our departed into your hands. We are filled with the sure hope that our departed will rise again on the Last Day with all who have died in Christ. We thank you for all the good things you have given during our departed's earthly life.

O Father, in your great mercy, accept our prayer that the Gates of Paradise may be opened for your servant. In our turn, may we too be comforted by the words of faith until we greet Christ in glory and are united with you and our departed.

Through Christ our Lord, Amen.

ETERNA – Series

The Resurrection Prayer dedicated to Gardner Fox. (Courtesy of Theresa Fox)

were informed by it.

The funeral was held on December 27 at St. James Church. They held a full Roman Catholic mass in his honor with a wake the night before. It was a closed-casket funeral because Lynda wanted people to remember her husband alive. There were a lot of people who came to say goodbye to him. The whole family showed, along with some cousins from his mother's side. A few of their neighbors from Yonkers made it, and all their new friends at Rossmoor were in attendance as well. Lynda was still grieving throughout the funeral; she cried profusely. Later, she had Gardner cremated. As of the 1960s, the Catholic Church permitted cremation on the grounds of the Biblical verse "ashes to ashes" and this is what both of them wanted done. His remains were interred in Jamesburg's Holy Cross Burial Park Mausoleum. At the age of 76, Lynda Fox died on December 10, 1991. She now rests beside her husband once more.

In an interview Fox did for *Comics Interview* in 1984, Lou Mougin asked about his plans for the future. Fox laughingly responded, "Loafing." According to then 73-year-old Fox, this meant writing a book a year, but knowing that it is all right if the book doesn't get done. The interview ended with Fox simply stating, "I want to enjoy life as it comes."[15] It took Fox a long time to get to that point. Luckily, his impressive work ethic drove him toward what he enjoyed.

The sword-and-sorcery genre was one he had been drawn to since he was eleven years old. He repeatedly tried to invoke the genre, starting in 1950 with the first Howardian fantasy feature, a three-issue series titled *Crom the Barbarian*, but nothing really took off. His later years happened to coincide with a fantasy boom where *Conan the Barbarian* became a popular movie and *Dungeons & Dragons* was taking off. This finally provided him the opportunity to fulfill his dream of creating a comparable hero. And create he did as he jumped from one fantasy hero to the next.

It wasn't just Fox who focused on these heroes during this boom. Roy Thomas turned Fox's popular Alan Morgan, the hero of his earlier paperback novel *Warrior of Llarn*, into a fanzine comic in 1965, although the comics version went unpublished until 1971, and adapted his second Kothar outing, *Kothar and the Conjurer's Curse,* into a six-part Marvel Conan story, starting with *Conan the Barbarian* #46 in 1975.

Fox was busy doing other work, too, with a string of spy novels in the *Lady from L.U.S.T.* series, the science fiction novel *Conehead,* his hardcover western *Carty,* and others. On top of all that, his final projects included a tabletop game and writing for Eclipse Comics, one of the independent comic publishers that started the industry-wide debate over creator rights. This eventually paved the way for companies, including DC, to revise their work-for-hire agreements, which would have appeased Fox's sense of justice and likely brought him catharsis after the defeat he suffered as part of the Writers' Strike in 1968. It is possible he could have had a full return after being inspired to write a new Hawkman tale, but it was simply not meant to be.

As busy as he stayed in these years, he made the time to witness how impressive his sister and children had become. With his wife by his side, he helped form adults who carried on the family tradition of giving back to the community, caring about education, and preserving history. This is perhaps his greatest achievement.

Gardner Fox followed his dreams until the end and made a positive impact on everyone around him, including his readers. His dream to make a man capable of standing among heroes came true. He just didn't know he was talking about himself.

CHAPTER FIFTEEN

Garnering a Grasp on Gardner Fox's Legacy

Gardner Fox started writing comics before the creation of Superman in the late 1930s and continued writing comics until the start of the creator-owned independent comics movement in the mid-1980s. By his own records, Fox wrote 4,213 comic book stories by 1980, making him the second most prolific writer in the medium, after Robert Kanigher.[16] During that time, Fox co-created dozens of long-running characters, re-invented many of them in the Silver Age, along with a few others, and wrote too many firsts to list. The majority of these characters were for DC, but Fox wrote for a large number of comic companies including EC, Magazine Enterprises, and Marvel. He greatly impacted the development of fan culture and attended early conventions as well. He even influenced the start of the role-playing game trend. The list of comics creators who are known fans of Gardner Fox is substantial, including Tim Truman, Roy Thomas, Michael T. Gilbert, Jerry Bails, Marv Wolfman, Mike Barr, Gil Kane, and Gerry Conway, as well as the "father of comics fandom," Dr. Jerry Bails.

With all these qualifiers, one would think he would be talked about far more than he is. Thankfully, there are a few points in time where people more actively sought to raise Fox's public recognition, such as shortly after his death, and now we are seeing it once again. With his characters and stories becoming increasingly mainstream, it is time for Gardner Fox to become the household name he should be.

After his death, several people in the comics industry mourned, with Mark Gruenwald and John Byrne writing two of the most relevant tributes. In one of Mark Gruenwald's famous "Mark's Remarks," found in 1987's *The Avengers* #282, he describes Gardner Fox's stories as masterpieces in his editorial comments that take up a full third of the letters page. He states that Fox's stories were capable of holding his childhood attention before he could fully understand the intricacies Fox worked into his plots. More than just a great writer, though, Gruenwald saw Gardner Fox as an inspirational master of the form and tells the story of when he made a physical trek to Fox's home in Yonkers to tell him so. In 1976, Gruenwald and three other comics fans knocked on his door and were treated to three hours of quality time reminiscing with the bemused Fox, who even took them upstairs on a tour to show them his home office where he wrote. Gruenwald described Fox as a kind, patient, and indulgent man. He left the Fox home assured in his dream to become a comic book writer like many of the other people Fox encouraged over the years.

Mark Gruenwald's final sentiments were: "Gardner F. Fox is gone, but his work will continue to influence succeeding generations of comic book writers. Mr. Fox's position as one of the major figures in early comics literature is assured."[17]

His work has indeed continued to influence people, even if people are not always aware it is Fox's work they are interacting with.

The disconnection between his name and his work is still something that must be overcome. This is something John Byrne touches on in his memoriam to Gardner Fox, which was published in 1987's *Action Comics* #589, and written one week after Fox's death. In it, Byrne explains that Fox was the first comic book writer he knew by name. Giving credit to writers was still a rarity when Byrne started reading comics, but, once he learned of Fox, he realized that all his favorite stories were written by the man. Byrne ended his memoriam by stating, "The body of work he left, the wonders he created, stand as a legacy to be cherished and, for those of us fortunate enough to follow in his footsteps, a legacy to be admired and envied."[18]

These last sentiments are especially poignant given the fact that Byrne had just moved from Marvel to DC after being hired to reinvent Superman. As part of his new origin miniseries, titled *Man of Steel,* Byrne was drawing on many of DC's classic characters, and the issue just prior to the one containing his memoriam included Hawkman and his wife. These winged wonders would soon be turned into yet another homage to Gardner Fox.

As a friend of Fox in his last years, Timothy Truman felt the need to memorialize him in the form of a three-issue mini-series titled *Hawkworld. Hawkman* had been one of the DC titles Truman had followed when growing up, and, after Frank Miller's recent success bringing Batman back to his darker Fox-and Finger-based roots, DC was looking to revitalize another character. Editor Mike Gold called on Truman to take on the task, and he knew just want to do. He and Gardner Fox had already discussed it during one of their many chats. Gold was a fan of Fox's work as well, so, when Truman told him he wanted to do a "contemporary tribute" to the recently deceased Fox, Gold was fully on board.[19]

Just before his death, Fox had described his dream project, and what would have been his final work: a Hawkman tale set on Thanagar and heavily influenced by Edgar Rice Burroughs's John Carter of Mars. In 1989, *Hawkworld* came out and it was written in the way that Truman believes Fox would have wanted it to be. In Truman's own words, "I don't know exactly what Gar had in mind for Hawkman, but my version was very much a tribute to him but with all these Truman-isms—my own interests—thrown in."[13]

Like many of Fox's more traditional heroes, Katar Hol is a young aristocratic "wingman" who turns his back on upper society to do his duty in the lowly Downside of Thanagar. Bringing the John Carter aspects into it, Truman wanted to make it feel like an epic action story set in a supposedly utopian fantasy world with added substance. Artist Enrique Alcatena helped capture this aesthetic well. Truman used Gardner Fox's choice to make Hawkman an archeologist as a main frame. It is through this drive for historical discovery that antiquated notions of honor are questioned, in a way that sounds comparable to what Fox was playing with before his death. Regardless, Hawkman's drive for justice prevails as he works to help those in need. This made the *Hawkworld* title fit in more with the modern trends being explored at DC, such as social inequality, something Fox exhibited in a lot of his work going all the way back to the 1940s.

It is safe to say that Gardner Fox would have approved. Whether fans were aware the miniseries was a tribute or not, the series sold well enough that it was extended to a monthly title. This was not the only work showing reverence to Fox.

Although many of Fox's stories remain largely uncredited to him, those who are aware of his contributions can spot a steady trickle of shout-outs and references across multiple mediums.

Starting with comics in the 60s, John Broome named not one but two characters after his writing companion: Green Lantern/Guy Gardner and Atomic Knight/Gardner Grayle. In the Bronze Age, Steve Englehart included a reference to Gardner Fox, along with nods to several other DC creators, in the form of the Fox Gardens restaurant in *Detective Comics* #474. Kurt Busiek has included multiple references including his backup series titled "Tiberius Fox" found in the black-and-white horror miniseries *Phantom of Fear City* from Claypool Comics, and the aptly named Fox-Broome University in *Astro City*.

Moving to another medium, the animated television series *Justice League* included a pair of episodes that were dedicated to Fox titled "Legends." They were written as an homage to Fox's annual Silver Age crossovers, which featured both the Justice Society of America and the Justice League of America. Likewise, the animated series titled Young Justice contains a moment where Flash directs a woman to a homeless shelter located on the cross streets of Gardner and Fox during a tropical storm. Those same cross streets appeared in the first episode of the *The Flash* television show from the 1990s. The newest *The Flash* show, on the CW, has brought many of the major storylines Fox was behind to a new generation and contains an abundance of Fox's lesser-known characters." They included a Gardner Fox Easter egg in the episode titled "The Present" where Barry Allen and Jay Garrick chat outside of Fox Bank after foiling the Trickster's attempt to rob it.

This list is not comprehensive, but it shows a number of creators giving Fox the credit he deserves. Unfortunately, all these nods are only understood if the reader or the viewer recognizes their significance. Sadly, many fans today have no idea who Gardner Fox is, while at the same time enjoying his work.

Even within the Fox family, his greatness needed to be taught and this, unfortunately, came with the knowledge that Fox was not getting his fair dues. While his children and grandchildren knew he was a writer, the humble Gardner rarely talked to them about writing or anything comic book related. Greg Fox wasn't fully aware of his grandfather's contributions until a friend from high school informed him. Mike Dass told him more "in one breath" about his grandfather's comic writing than he had ever known before that point.[20]

Theresa Fox had a similar experience when she was on a French tour bus with some high school groups in 1989. They were crossing the French countryside when she mentioned she was related to a writer while talking to a knowledgeable comic book fan from Tennessee. When she said it was Gardner Fox, he "flew" about five seats to talk with her.[21] It seemed a little crazy to her when he revealed he had a shrine to her grandfather in his room, but she couldn't wait to go home and tell her family about the encounter. This lack of knowledge was not necessarily on purpose.

Gardner Fox won a few posthumous awards, but his children Jefferey and Lynda felt strange about attending such events and so didn't. This meant the family didn't attend when he won a Harvey Award for his career body of work, nor when he was entered into the Jack Kirby Hall of Fame in 1998. Similarly, they did not represent him when he was inducted into the Eisner Award Hall of Fame a year later. A bigger reason why they stayed home was their health. Most notably, Lynda Fox-Cohen was suffering through a long battle with pancreatic cancer at the time she was invited to celebrate her father when he was given the Bill Finger Award for Excellence in Comic Book Writing in 2007. (Lynda died on March 1, 2008.) Jeffrey Fox suffered from COPD, making travel difficult in general. (He died on December 26, 2012.) The rest of the family did not know Gardner was receiving this recognition and the grandchildren were horrified to learn his memory was not being honored by the family during these times. It seemed as though they would have to accept that he was destined to be an unsung hero.

The rise of the internet created the opportunity for fans to more easily share their love of Gardner Fox along with his and characters. Kurt Brugel is running a Fox-dedicated Twitter account, Facebook page, and starting conversations about him on Goodreads. Howard Moses shares whole comic books written by Fox on Brugel's Facebook page. Another major supporter of Fox, Tim Board, moderates a Hawkman page and encourages fans to celebrate Hawkman Day on November 10.

Somebody who has supported this spreading of knowledge in a more indirect manner is playwright Lenny Schwartz, who wrote a play, that is posted to Youtube, about Bill Finger, titled "Co-Creator: The Man Behind the Bat." Bill Finger's story is deeply depressing. He is responsible for much of what we think of when it comes to Batman, but he died poor and alone after receiving little recognition. Gardner Fox, a friend of Finger's, was particularly aware of this mistreatment of a fellow early writer of Batman. Fox wasn't a firebrand, but he sought to remedy this injustice when and where he could. Lenny Schwartz included Fox as a character in his play, and it is reasonable to believe that Fox certainly would have been proud to support his friend achieving the legacy he deserves. Schwartz used the transcripts from the New York City comic convention panel from in 1965 to inform his portrayal of Fox and, using the language of Fox's family, described Fox as another "unsung hero of comics."[22] Finger now shares credit with Bob Kane and this is even more important in our present day given how popular super-hero movies have become.

The 2018 movie *Justice League* garnered mixed reviews, but it marks a pivotal shift in the story of Gardner Fox. Fox did not get to see his name credited when his story "The Remarkable Ruse of the Riddler," from *Batman* #171, was adapted into the two-part series opener for the *Batman* television show in 1966. This cannot be righted, but his family did get to see him receive just credit for his writing of the JLA in the *Justice League* movie. DC offered the family tickets to the premier, and Theresa Fox took them up on their offer. She brought along her husband and her sister, Deborah Fox. It was quite the step up from their previous plans to watch the movie together at the local theater. They got to hang out on the red carpet and were ushered in to sit with the DC heir's representative and his wife, who pointed out the other grandkids in attendance. Everyone stayed to watch the end credits, so they all saw Gardner Fox cited as a creator on the big screen in the Kodak Theater. This proved a defining moment when it comes to his creative legacy and it was most certainly pleasing to both his family and his fans. The Fox family was also invited to the after party, which revealed more delights.

Theresa Fox had a particularly worthwhile chat with actor Ezra Miller, who played the Flash. As it turns out, he is a huge Gardner Fox fan. This was rewarding to know for the Fox family, as they felt Miller conveyed true appreciation for Fox's creative process. He told them there were nods to Gardner Fox that were later edited out of the movie. These cuts are made more disappointing by the fact that Fox did not get the same kind of credit for his co-creation of the Flash. Still, the Fox family was proud to be able to bear witness to something Fox himself did not get to see.

On top of the entertainment value Gardner Fox brought to his comics, he also included many educative facts and humanitarian lessons, and he is finally getting his due credit through his college as well. Fox's comics were filled with specific and accurate information across a breadth of disciplines including literature, history, science, mythology, and ethics. Learning something new everyday was one of the primary drives Fox exhibited, and he shared that knowledge in his writing. This helped educate his readers at the same time he educated himself. This was never more important than when he was writing stories promoting the equal treatment of women and minorities. Another way he actively supported and encouraged those who love and want to study comic books was to donate his files, including comics, correspondence, and manuscripts, to the University of Oregon in Eugene, OR.

This book would have been substantially harder to write without that donation, and the archive means that others can work on his materials as well.

Early in the process of writing this book, I wanted to attain Fox's college transcripts and this resulted in the family realizing St. John's University did not have him listed as one of their notable alumni. Despite the fact that their alumni magazines were regularly listing Fox's books in their pages while he was alive, even his college had overlooked him. This realization prompted Theresa Fox, who has taken over the role of keeping Gardner Fox's memory alive, much like her aunt Lynda Fox-Cohen did before her, to work with the university to get him the credit he so deserves.

The endeavor was successful and St. John's University sent the family a letter stating, "Mr. Fox indeed represented St. John's to the highest level with his many professional and personal accomplishments. Students and fellow colleagues were so interested in his life and his amazing legacy as word made around the office."[23]

When we consider how many years he paid alumni dues, and the effort he took to keep the school up to date with his accomplishments, it suggests this achievement would mean just as much to him as the recognition he receives for his comic work.

Gardner Fox regularly urged his readers to treat others in a just and fair manner. With so many accomplishments, it is just and fair for his name to be included alongside the other comics greats. Much like in the 1960s and 1970s, during the rise of fanzines like *Alter-Ego* (the hyphen was dropped in 1963), people are currently fighting for just that.

Fox was an erudite individual and encouraged this type of research when he donated his materials to the University of Oregon. He believed it was possible to read his work through a scholarly lens, and enjoyed it when fans wanted to have intellectual conversations about his work. These conversations can only be had if his name reaches the cultural milieu his better known colleagues share.

His daughter, Lynda Fox-Cohen, spoke of him in a letter to Paul Kupperberg: "I've always felt that he was very, very special; when I feel 'off' I think of his blue eyes twinkling. It is very important to me to have his memory kept alive. The grandchildren will know him through us."[24]

With Hawkman in his own title again, the Justice League in movie theaters, and the Flash on television screens, it is the perfect time to draw more awareness to his contributions.

It's time for Gardner Fox to be seen as the all-star he truly is.

Notes

Introduction

1 I largely refer to the various companies that were under the umbrella of DC or purchased by DC as DC for simplicity's sake. This is also to prevent any possible confusion when Fox is working for companies outside of what I am referring to as simply DC.

2 Fox, Gardner. Received by Jerry Bails. 31 January 1959.

3 "Gardner Fox Adventures" *Batmania* #22. 1977. Gardner Fox literary manuscripts, comic books, and other material, Coll 008, Special Collections & University Archives, University of Oregon Libraries, Eugene, Oregon.

4 Codieck, Barrett. "Gardner Fox literary manuscripts, comic books and other material, 1936-1978." Archives West <http://archiveswest.orbiscascade.org/ark:/80444/xv29623>

5 Fox, Gardner. "The Life and Good Times of Gardner F. Fox: A Letter from the Co-Creator of Flash and Hawkman." *Alter Ego*. Ed. Roy Thomas, TwoMorrows Publishing, 2000, pp. 22-25.

6 Gilbert, Michael. "The Fox and the Fans: Letters to Gardner F. Fox from Future Pros—1959-1965" *Alter Ego—The Comic Book Artist Collection*. Ed. Roy Thomas, TwoMorrows Publishing, 2001, pp. 17-21.

Part One

1 "Behind the Swords." *Star Studded Comics* No. 17. 1971. Gardner Fox literary manuscripts, comic books, and other material, Coll 008, Special Collections & University Archives, University of Oregon Libraries, Eugene, Oregon.

2 "1906 DeBris." PUD00019. Debris Yearbooks, Purdue University. Purdue University Libraries, Archives and Special Collections. Purdue University, West Lafayette, IN. http://earchives.lib.purdue.edu/cdm/compoundobject/collection/debris/id/ 9496/rec/1. Accessed 20 Nov. 2017.

3 Fox, Theresa. "My mother's answers" Message to Jennifer DeRoss. 17 Jan. 2018.

4 Fox, Greg. "Gardner Fox." Message to Jennifer DeRoss. 21 February 2017. E-mail.

5 "CPI Inflation Calculator." United States Department of Labor, https://www.bls.gov/data/inflation_calculator.htm. Accessed 29 Jan. 2018.

6 "From out of the Past." *Remember When* #4. 1972. 1. Gardner Fox literary manuscripts, comic books, and other material, Coll 008, Special Collections & University Archives, University of Oregon Libraries, Eugene, Oregon.

7 Fox, Gardner. "Under the Sorcerer's Spell," *All-Flash*. vol 1, no. 15, DC Comics,1944, pp. 16-28.

8 "2 College Students Fined for Having Guns" *The Brooklyn Daily Eagle*, 01 Dec 1929, B3.

9 *Vincentian* 1932, St. John's University Archives, Queens, New York.

10 Commencement of St. John's College 1932, St. John's University Archives, Queens, New York.

11 Kocak, Tyler. "Re: Gardner Fox." Message to Jennifer DeRoss. 31 July 2017.

12 "About Phi Delta Phi International." *Phi Delta Phi: The international Legal Honor Society*, http://www.phideltaphi.org/?page=About. Accessed 31 Jan. 2018.

13 Garvey, Ellen Gruber. *Writing with Scissors: American Scrapbooks from the Civil War to the Harlem Renaissance*. Oxford University Press, 2013.

14 Scrapbook. Gardner Fox literary manuscripts, comic books, and other material, Coll 008, Special Collections & University Archives, University of Oregon Libraries, Eugene, Oregon.

15 "265 Boro, L.I. Residents Are Admitted to Bar" *The Brooklyn Daily Eagle*, 19 Aug 1935.

16 Fox, Gardner. Letter to Roy Thomas. 13 March 1965. Gardner Fox literary manuscripts, comic books, and other material, Coll 008, Special Collections & University Archives, University of Oregon Libraries, Eugene, Oregon.

Part Two

1 Fox, Theresa. "Questions about Gardner Fox." Received by Jennifer DeRoss, 14 February 2017.

2 Mougin, Lou. Interview with Gardner Fox. *Comics Interview* vol. 1, no. 9, 1984, pp. 15-22.

3 Fox, Gardner. Received by Roy Thomas. 13 March 1965. Gardner Fox literary manuscripts, comic books, and other material, Coll 008, Special Collections & University Archives, University of Oregon Libraries, Eugene, Oregon.

4 Armstrong, David. "In Search of Bert Christman: The Short and Adventurous Life of the Man Who Created 'The Sandman'" *Alter Ego* #45. Ed. Roy Thomas, TwoMorrows Publishing, 2005. pp. 18-35.

5 Amash, Jim. "'What Led You to Get a Job in Comic Books?' 'Hunger! What Else?': Comic Pioneer Greig Flessel Talks about the Golden Age— And Before!"*Alter Ego* #45. Ed. Roy Thomas. TwoMorrows Publishing, 2005, pp. 3-17.

6 Yet another writer who did not receive credit for the writing of Batman in the 40s was Ruth "Bunny" Lyons Kaufman. It is very likely that she is the first female to ever write for Batman. For more information, check out Bill Jourdain's "I Wrote Batman in the 1940s!" *Alter Ego* #27. vol 3, no. 27, 2003, 38-41.

7 Weldon, Glen. *The Caped Crusade: Batman and the Rise of Nerd Culture.* Simon & Schuster, 2017.

8 "Gardner Fox Adventures" *Batmania* #22. 1977. Gardner Fox literary manuscripts, comic books, and other material, Coll 008, Special Collections & University Archives, University of Oregon Libraries, Eugene, Oregon.

9 Daniel, Les. *DC Comics: A Celebration of the Worlds Favorite Comic Book Heroes.* Billboard Books, 2003.

10 Memo. Gardner Fox literary manuscripts, comic books, and other material, Coll 008, Special Collections & University Archives, University of Oregon Libraries, Eugene, Oregon.

11 Program for Comicon 1965. Gardner Fox literary manuscripts, comic books, and other material, Coll 008, Special Collections & University Archives, University of Oregon Libraries, Eugene, Oregon.

12 Fox, Gardner. "The Flash." *Flash Comics*, vol. 1, no. 1, DC Comics, 1940, pp. 3-17.

13 This was also informed by his personal experience. St. John's Law permitted the enrollment of diverse students including women and minorities. Gardner Fox's graduating class contained three women.

14 Brooker, Will. "Fandom and Authorship." *The Super-hero Reader*, Ed. Charles Hatfield, Jeet Heer, and Kent Worcester, University Press of Mississippi, 2013, pp. 61-71.

15 Fox, Gardner. "The Hawkman." *Flash Comics*, vol. 1, no. 1, DC Comics, 1940, pp. 24-35.

16 Tollin, Anthony. "Origins of the Golden Age." *Amazing World of DC Comics* no. 5: Sheldon Mayer The Man Behind the Golden Age, vol. 2, no. 5, DC Comics, 1975, pp. 2-11.

17 "Ghost Writers In The Sky: The-ever 'Creators Panel' at a Comics Convention—Featuring Otto Binder, Gardner Fox, Bill Finger, & Mort Weisinger." *Alter Ego*. Trans. Tim Easterday. Ed. Roy Thomas. TwoMorrows Publishing, 2003. pp. 9-29.

18 Laurence R. D'Orsay ephemera. Gardner Fox literary manuscripts, comic books, and other material, Coll 008, Special Collections & University Archives, University of Oregon Libraries, Eugene, Oregon.

19 Fox, Gardner. "Introducing America's National Hero! The Skyman" *The Skyman* no. 1, Columbia, 1941, pp. 3- 17.

20 Fox, Gardner. "Doctor Fate" *The Golden Age Doctor Fate—Archives Volume 1* DC Comics, 2007, 11-16.

21 Thomas, Roy. "Re: Researching Gardner Fox." Message to Jennifer DeRoss. 3 November 2015.

22 Tollin, Anthony. "Origins of the Golden Age: Sheldon Mayer" Amazing World of DC Comics #5: Sheldon Mayer The Man Behind the Golden Age, vol. 2, no. 5, DC Comics, 1975, pp. 2-11.

23 "Distinguished Letters" *Paul Kupperberg: And then I wrote*. https://kupps.malibulist.com/2015/10/30/distinguished-letters/. Accessed 4 May 2018.

Part Three

1 Mougin, Lou. Interview with Gardner Fox. *Comics Interview* vol. 1, no. 9, 1984, pp. 15-22.

2 Fox, Gardner. "Food For Starving Patriots!" *All Star Comics— Archives, Volume 3*, DC Comics, 1997, pp.182-237.

3 Fox, Greg. "Re: Gardner Fox Questions." Received by Jennifer DeRoss, 12 February 2017.

4 Kimble, James J. and Goodnow, Trischa. "Introduction." *The 10¢ War: Comic Books, Propaganda, and World War II*, University Press of Mississippi, 2016, pp. 3-25.

5 Fox, Gardner. "The Man Who Relived His Life!" *All-Star Comics*. vol. 2, no. 21, All American Publications, 1944.

6 Tuttle, William M.. "Children's Entertainment: Radio, Movies, Comics." *Daddy's Gone to War: The Second World War in the Lives of America's Children*, edited by GB Cary, Oxford University Press, 1993, pp. 148-161.

7 "Memo," Gardner Fox literary manuscripts, comic books, and other material, Coll 008, Special Collections & University Archives, University of Oregon Libraries, Eugene, Oregon.

8 Murray, Christopher. *Champions of the Oppressed?: Super-hero Comics, Popular Culture, and Propaganda in America During World War II*, Hamption Press, INC. 2011.

9 "Vincentian Heritage." *St. John's University*, http://www.stjohns. edu/about/vincentian-heritage. Accessed on 17 February 2017.

10 "1000 At Mission Crusade Party." *The Brooklyn Daily Eagle*, 09 November 1929. "Fourth Bridge Dance." The Brooklyn Daily Eagle, 01 November 1931.

11 Fox, Gardner. "Food For Starving Patriots!" *All Star Comics—Archives, Volume 3*, DC Comics, 1997, pp. 182-237.

12 Thomas, Roy. "Forward: 'This Means War!:' A Personal and Historical Note." *All Star Comics—Archives, Volume 3*, DC Comics, 1997, pp. 1-5.

13 Whitney Ellsworth and Murray Bonltinoff. "Helpful Hints." 16 October 1940. Gardner Fox literary manuscripts, comic books, and other material, Coll 008, Special Collections & University Archives, University of Oregon Libraries, Eugene, Oregon.

14 Fox, Gardner. "This is our Enemy!" *All Star Comics*, vol. 2, no. 24, All American Publications, 1945.

15 "Gardner Fox Adventures" *Batmania* #22. 1977. Gardner Fox literary manuscripts, comic books, and other material, Coll 008, Special Collections & University Archives, University of Oregon Libraries, Eugene, Oregon.

16 Fox, Gardner. "Flash Comics #2." *The Golden Age Hawkman - Archives Volume 1*, DC Comics, 2005, pp. 22-33.

17 Daniels, Les. *The Life and Times of the Amazon Princess Wonder Woman: The Complete History*. Chronicle Books LLC, 2000.

18 Saunders, Ben. "Wonder Woman: Bondage and Liberation." *Do The Gods Wear Capes?: Spirituality, Fantasy, and Super-heroes*, Bloomsbury Academic, 2011, pp. 36-71.

19 Fox, Gardner. "The Justice Society Joins the War on Japan!" *All Star Comics—Archives, Volume 3*, DC Comics, 1997, 2007, pp. 182-237.

20 Thomas, Roy. "Two Touches of Venus: Wonder Woman Gets 'Shanghaied Into Space;—Twice Over" *The Alter Ego Collection Volume 1*, TwoMorrows Publishing, 1999, pp. 60-70.

21 Kanigher, Robert. "Kanigher on Kanigher (and Everything Else!): A Long Letter from "RK"—and Ye Editor's response." *The Alter Ego Collection Volume 1*, TwoMorrows Publishing, 1999, pp. 169-172.

22 *All-Star Comics* vol. 1, no. 5, All American Publications, 1941, pp. 64.

23 *All-Star Comics* vol.1, no. 5, All American Publications, 1941, pp. 64. 27 Fox, Gardner. "The Black Dragon Menace" *All Star Comics—Archives Volume 3*, DC Comics, 2007, pp. 68-123.

24 MacDonald, Heidi. "How a toxic history of harassment has damaged the comics industry." *The Beat: The News Blog on Comics Culture*. http://www.comicsbeat.com/how-a-toxic-history-of-harass-ment-has-damaged-the-comics-industry/. Accessed 15 May 2018

25 Smith, Matthew J. "Working Girl: Diana Prince and the Crisis of Career Moves" *The Ages of Wonder Woman: Essays on the Amazon Princess in Changing Times*, McFarland, 2013, pp. 151-162.

Part Four

1 Schelly, Bill. *Man of Rock: A Biography of Joe Kubert*. Fantographics Books, 2008.

2 "Writing Schedule" 1945. Gardner Fox literary manuscripts, comic books, and other material, Coll 008, Special Collections & University Archives, University of Oregon Libraries, Eugene, Oregon.

3 Schwartz, Julius and Brian M. Thomsen. *Man of Two Worlds: My Life in Science Fiction and Comics*. HarperEntertainment, 2000.

4 Fox, Gardner, "The Weirds of the Woodcarver" *Weird Tales* vol. 38, no. 1, 1944. pp. 76-81.

5 "Business Correspondence" 1951.Gardner Fox literary manuscripts, comic books, and other material, Coll 008, Special Collections & University Archives, University of Oregon Libraries, Eugene, Oregon.

6 Michael T. Gilbert goes over how these formulas work and where they be seen across Gardner Fox's canon in "Nuts and Bolts! The Gardner Fox Scrapbook Chapter II" from *Alter Ego* Vol. 3, No. 21, 2003.

7 Fox, Gardner. *The Borgia Blade*. Fawcett Publications, 1953.

8 Seuling, Phil. Interview with Gardner Fox. New York Comic Art Convention. Transcribed by John Benson. 1971.

9 Leon Fox. Received by Gardner Fox. 1 May 1953.

10 Julia Gardner. Received by "Dear Ones." 11 June 1953.

11 Fox-Cohen, Lynda."Re:Writer's"strike"of1967-"Message to Roy Thomas. 19 April 2002.

12 *Redman* 1953, St. John's University Archives, Queens, New York.

13 "Gardner Fox Adventures," *Batmania* #22, 1977. Gardner Fox literary manuscripts, comic books, and other material, Coll 008, Special Collections & University Archives, University of Oregon Libraries, Eugene, Oregon.

14 Fox, Gardner. *Moon Girl Fights Crime*, vol. 1, no. 7, Entertaining Comics. 1949.

15 Tilley, Carol. "Seducing the Innocent: Fredric Wertham and the Falsifications that Helped Condemn Comics." *Alter Ego*, vol. 3, no. 128, Ed. Roy Thomas, TwoMorrows Publishing, 2014. pp. 3-29.

16 Albrechts, Christian. "Ideology and Power in Pre-Code Comic Books: Struggles for Cultural Space, Audience, and Meaning." Dissertation, Kiel University, 2012.

17 Latona, Robert. Fan letter. Gardner Fox literary manuscripts, comic books, and other material, Coll 008, Special Collections & University Archives, University of Oregon Libraries, Eugene, Oregon.

18 Thomas, Roy."Re:Researching Gardner Fox."Message to Jennifer DeRoss. 3 August 2016.

19 "The Beautiful Witch" *Ghost Rider*, vol. 1, no. 11, Magazine Enterprises, 1953, pp. 2-8.

20 Green, Paul. *Encyclopedia of Weird Westerns*, McFarland & Company Inc, 2009.

21 Thomas, Roy. "Thanks For Nothing!" *Alter Ego*, vol. 3, no. 128, Ed. Roy Thomas, TwoMorrows Publishing, 2014. pp. 2.

22 Fox, Gardner. "Secret of the Sinister Sorcerers!" *Justice League of America*, vol. 1, no. 2, National Periodical Publications, 1960.

Part Five

1 Bails, Jerry. Received by Gardner Fox. 24 June 1960.

2 "Gardner Fox Adventures." *Batmania* #22. 1977. Gardner Fox literary manuscripts, comic books, and other material, Coll 008, Special Collections & University Archives, University of Oregon Libraries, Eugene, Oregon.

3 Barr, Mike W. "Adam Strange." *The Silver Age Sci-Fi Companion*, 2007, pp. 28-59.

4 Gerard Jones and Will Jacobs. *The Comic Book Heroes: From the Silver Age to the Present*. Prima Lifestyles. 1996.

5 Jerry Bails. Received by Gardner Fox. 1961.

6 George Bammer. Received by Gardner Fox. 6 March 1966.

7 Letter from Jim Hendryx. 30 July 1952. Gardner Fox literary manuscripts, comic books, and other material, Coll 008, Special Collections & University Archives, University of Oregon Libraries, Eugene, Oregon.

8 Fox, Gardner. "Man, Thy Name Is—Brother!" *Justice League of America*, vol. 1, no. 57, National Periodical Publications, 1967, pp. 2-27.

9 Fox, Gardner. "Challenge of the Untouchable Aliens!" *Justice League of America*, vol. 1, no. 15, National Periodical Publications, 1962, pp. 3-31.

10 Fawaz, Ramzi. "The Family of Superman: The Super-hero Team and the Promise of Universal Citizenship." *The New Mutants: Super-heroes and the Radical Imagination of American Comics*. New York University Press, 2016. pp. 37-65.

11 Wright, Fredrick A, "I Can Pass Right Through Solid Matter!": How the Flash Upheld American Values While Breaking the Speed Limit." *Comic Books and the Cold War: Essays on Graphic Treatment of Communism, the Code and Social Concerns*. Ed. Chris York and Rafeil York. McFarland & Company, Inc, 2012. pp. 55- 67.

12 Fox, Theresa. "Fw: Questions about Gardner Fox." Message to Jennifer DeRoss. 20 February 2017.

13 Lynda Fox-Cohen. "Re:" *Alter Ego*, vol. 3, no. 12, TwoMorrows Publishing, 2002, pp. 33-35.

14 Barr, Mike W. "Spotlight on 'The Strange Adventure That Really Happened!'" *The Silver Age Sci-Fi Companion*, 2007, pp. 106-117.

15 Mitchell, A.A. "Distributed Identity: Networking Image Fragments in Graphic Memoirs." *Studies in Comics*, vol. 1, no. 2, 2010, pp. 257-279.

16 Fox, Gardner. "The Strange Death of Batman—Chapter 2," *Detective Comics*, vol. 1, no. 347, National Periodical Publications, 1966, pp. 14-19.

17 Fox, Gardner. "The Life and Good Times of Gardner F. Fox: A Letter form the Co-Creator of Flash and Hawkman." *Alter Ego*, vol. 3, no 4, Ed. Roy Thomas, TwoMorrow Publishing, 2000, pp. 22-25.

18 Eury, Michael. "Bragging Rights: How Justice League of America Inspired the Marvel Universe" *The Justice League Companion*. TwoMorrows Publishing, 2005. pp. 28-31.

19 Lillian III, Guy H. "Strange Schwartz Stories." *Amazing World of DC Comics*. vol. 1, no. 3, DC Comics, 1974, pp. 2-11.

20 White slavery is not something most would include in a list of relevant issues. That said, it provides a range of relevancy that proves his argument. White Slavery is no longer an issue that can be considered relevant. The topic likely came to mind because Gardner Fox wrote about white slavery in 1955's *Barbary Slave*.

21 Seuling, Phil. Interview with Gardner Fox. New York Comic Art Convention. Transcribed by John Benson. 1971.

22 Bails, Jerry. Received by Gardner Fox. 6 September 1953.

23 Fox, Gardner. Received by Jerry Bails. 31 January 1959.

24 Thomas, Roy. Received by Gardner Fox. 21 November 1960. Gardner Fox literary manuscripts, comic books, and other material, Coll 008, Special Collections & University Archives, University of Oregon Libraries, Eugene, Oregon.

25 Lupoff, Richard. Received by Gardner Fox. 16 January 1961. Gardner Fox literary manuscripts, comic books, and other material, Coll 008, Special Collections & University Archives, University of Oregon Libraries, Eugene, Oregon.

26 Brooker, Will. "Fandom and Authorship." *The Super-hero Reader*, Ed. Charles Hatfield, Jeet Heer, and Kent Worcester, University Press of Mississippi, 2013, pp. 61-71.

27 Fox, Gardner. Received by Jerry Bails. 10 April 1961.

28 *The Comic Reader* #45. 1966. Gardner Fox literary manuscripts, comic books, and other material, Coll 008, Special Collections & University Archives, University of Oregon Libraries, Eugene, Oregon.

29 "Alumni Gazette." *St. John's University Alumni News* vol 6, no. 4, 1964, pp. 4.

30 "Ghost Writers in The Sky: The First-Ever 'Creators Panel' at a Comics Convention—Featuring Otto Binder, Gardner Fox, Bill Finger,

& Mort Weisinger." *Alter Ego*. vol. 3, no. 20, Trans. Tim Easterday. Ed. Roy Thomas, TwoMorrows Publishing, 2003, pp. 9-29.

31 Schelly, Bill. "A Full-Service New York Comics Convention-Hurrah!: Alter Ego Revisits the First "Complete" Comiccon!" *Alter Ego* vol. 3, no. 20, TwoMorrows Publishing, 2003. pp. 5-8.

32 Schelly, Bill. Otto Binder: *The Life and Work of a Comic Book and Science Fiction Visionary*. North Atlantic Books. 2003.

33 Fox, Gardner. "The True-False Face of Batman." *Detective Comics*, vol. 1, no. 363, National Periodical Publications, 1967.

34 Rumrill, Alan F. Received by Jennifer DeRoss. 21 April 2017.

35 Fox, Gardner. "Batgirl's Costume Cut-Ups!" *Detective Comics*, vol. 1, no. 371, National Periodical Publications, 1968.

36 Mougin, Lou. Interview with Gardner Fox. *Comics Interview* vol. 1, no. 9, 1984, pp. 15-22.

37 John Broome left DC over a dispute about being paid for reprints around the same time as the Writer's Strike.

38 Seuling, Phil. Interview with Gardner Fox. New York Comic Art Convention. Transcribed by John Benson. 1971.

39 Thomas, Roy. "Guest of Honor Gardner Fox." New York City Con Program. 1971.

40 Morrissey, Richard H. *YZNGATZ* vol. 1, no. 3, 1976. pp. 2-5. Gardner Fox literary manuscripts, comic books, and other material, Coll 008, Special Collections & University Archives, University of Oregon Libraries, Eugene, Oregon.

41 Thomas, Roy. "Re: Researching Gardner Fox." Message to Jennifer DeRoss. 3 November 2015.

42 Horn, Maurice. *Comics of the American West*. Winchester Press, 1977.

43 Fox, Greg. "Gardner Fox." Message to Jennifer DeRoss. 21 February 2017.

44 Fox, Greg. "Re: Gardner Fox Questions Round 2." Message to Jennifer DeRoss. 3 December 2018

45 Feild, Tom. "Bring on the Bad Guys: The Tomb of Dracula" *Back Issue*, vol 1, no. 6, 2004, pp. 19-32.

46 Thomas, Roy. "Re: Researching Gardner Fox." Message to Jennifer DeRoss. 3 November 2015.

Part Six

1 "Behind the Swords." *Star Studded*, no. 17, 1971. Gardner Fox literary manuscripts, comic books, and other material, Coll 008, Special Collections & University Archives, University of Oregon Libraries, Eugene, Oregon.

2 Seuling, Phil. Interview with Gardner Fox. New York Comic Art Convention. Transcribed by John Benson. 1971.

3 Sinclair, Stéfan and Geoffrey Rockwell. Voyant Tools. Web. http://voyant-tools.org/, 2016.

4 Fox, Gardner. Received by Roy Thomas. 27 October 1980.

5 Fox, Greg. "Re: Gardner Fox Questions." Message to Jennifer DeRoss, 12 February 2017.

6 Peery, Susan M. *Our Window to a Wider World: An Informal History of Keen Public Library.* Keene New Hampshire Prospect Park Press. 2006.

7 "Longtime Librarian Dies." *Sentinel* [Keene NH], 10 August 1993. 7 Fox, Greg. "Re: Gardner Fox Questions Round 2." Message to Jennifer DeRoss. 3 December 2018

8 Fox, Greg. "Re: Gardner Fox Questions Round 2." Message to Jennifer DeRoss. 3 December 2018

9 Fox, Kenneth W. "Jeffrey F. Fox Obituary Memories and Candles." 28 December 2012, http://www.tributes.com/obituary/show/Jeffrey-F.-Fox-94981789. Accessed 11 May 2018.

10 Fox, Theresa. "For you...." Message to Jennifer DeRoss. 8 December 2018.

11 Fox, Gardner. Received by Roy Thomas. 27 October 1980.

12 "A Very Special Letter From Outside" Richard H. Morrissey *YZNG-ATZ*, no. 3 1976, pp. 1. Gardner Fox literary manuscripts, comic books, and other material, Coll 008, Special Collections & University Archives, University of Oregon Libraries, Eugene, Oregon.

13 Truman, Timothy. "Re: Gardner Fox." Message to Jennifer DeRoss. 23 April 2018.

14 Fox, Gardner, "From out of the Past." *Remember When* no. 4, 1972, pp. 1. Gardner Fox literary manuscripts, comic books, and other material, Coll 008, Special Collections & University Archives, University of Oregon Libraries, Eugene, Oregon.

15 Mougin, Lou. Interview with Gardner Fox. *Comics Interview* vol. 1, no. 9, 1984, pp. 15-22.

16 Fox, Gardner. Received by Roy Thomas. 27 October 1980.

17 Gruenwald, Mark. "Mark's Remarks." *Avengers*, vol. 1, no. 282, Marvel, 1987. pp. 23.

18 Byrne, John. "In Memoriam." *Action Comics*, vol. 1, no. 589, DC Comics, 1987, pp. 25.

19 Wilber, Steven. "Exploring Hawkworld." *Back Issue*, vol. 1, no. 97, 2017, pp. 23-30.

20 Fox, Greg. "Re: Gardner Fox Questions Round 2." Message to Jennifer DeRoss. 3 December 2018

21 Fox, Theresa. "Gardner Fox Questions Part 2." Message to Jennifer DeRoss. 27 October 2018.

22 Schwartz, Lenny. "Co-Creator." Message to Jennifer DeRoss. 11 November 2018.

23 Andrews, Mark. "Dear Fox Family." Received by "Fox Family." 14 December 2018.

24 "Distinguished Letters" Paul Kupperberg: And then I wrote. https:// kupps.malibulist.com/2015/10/30/distinguished-letters/. Accessed 4 May 2018.

Acknowledgments

If it wasn't for a number of people along the way, I never could have imagined I would be putting this book out in the world. The first two people I will always thank are my beloved children: Jacob and Cannon. Throughout this experience, their patience, understanding, and encouragement has made me more appreciative than they will ever know. My work is forever in dedication to them.

Another person who has more than earned my eternal gratefulness is Roy Thomas. This all started with a grad school project on Gardner Fox's scrapbook. I quickly saw a gap in the scholarship and was given his email as a supplemental source. Right from the start, he proved to be more than helpful and encouraging. I doubt I would have ever thought to take this project so far if it had not been for him. Similarly, Ben Saunders believed in me far before I believed in myself. I could never fully convey how thankful I am to him. As my primary mentor in relation to this project, Heidi Kaufman helped me navigate waters I never dreamt of treading, one of which was the undertaking of a master's thesis on the topic of Gardner Fox and his writing of Wonder Woman. The other members of my committee, Betsy Wheeler and Andréa Gilroy, more than earned my acknowledgment as well.

When it comes to helping with the day to day, Beverly Schlegel is deserving of my thanks in so many ways, from cooking dinner for the family to letting me talk out whatever part of the book I was working through. Tucker Mollers was also superb at offering different forms of support, and his keen eyes proved to be particularly worthy of my gratefulness. Offering consistent moral support and help along the way Wesley Peal, Ashley Darrow, and Shane Tydeman are all deserving of my thanks as well. I feel so lucky to have these wonderful people in my life.

Unsurprisingly, writing this book introduced me to new people. The Fox family was instrumental in making this book what it is. I want to thank Greg Fox, Martha Fox, and Theresa Fox, especially. Another big debt of gratitude goes out to Richard Fowlks, who blew me away with his cover designs and proved to be a pleasure to work with. Kurt Brugel gets a shout out for providing me with the necessary raw text to run Gardner Fox's novels through Voyant. I also wish to thank Gerry Conway, Paul Levitz, Michael T. Gilbert, Mike W. Barr, and Timothy Truman. Some of them helped me significantly more than others, but they were all willing to reply to my emails with kindness and support. For being willing to take a chance on me, I cannot forget a big thank you to my publisher, Bob McLain.

Finally, I want to thank all my friends on Twitter for enthusiastically cheering me on. And, to anybody still reading this, thank YOU!

About the Author

Jennifer DeRoss was born in San Jose, California, but spent most of her formative years in the foothills of the Sierra Nevadas. Living without electricity until the age of nine, reading was a main source of entertainment and comic books were included in her reading materials right from the start.

As an adult, she moved to Eugene, Oregon, and earned her master's degree at the University of Oregon, where she studied comics with a main focus on the modern American superhero. Her other fields of focus include queer studies, television studies, and biographical studies.

She is currently a proud mother of two boys and working as an instructional specialist at Lane Community College, where she is helping to develop and implement an early outreach and referral program to better ensure student success.

In addition, she co-founded, and contributes to, the female-led fandom website Sirens of Sequentials. She has previously written pieces on *Swamp Thing*, *Buffy the Vampire Slayer*, *Orphan Black*, and *Bitch Planet*.

CPSIA information can be obtained
at www.ICGtesting.com
Printed in the USA
LVHW081611090220
646330LV00008B/240